the garden sanctuary

keith mitchell

the garden sanctuary

Creating outdoor space to soothe the soul

hamlyn

CONTENTS

4

FIRST WORD

6

SEASONAL GARDENS

—

A Natural Calendar
describes the cycle of the
seasons and their
practical associations and
folklore connections.
With seasonal keynotes,
activities and insights,
garden tasks and ways to
encourage wildlife.

10

FEED THE SENSES

—

The garden as therapy
and inspiration through
colour, aroma, touch, taste
and sound, with planting
directories and design
ideas.

32

THE HEALING GARDEN

—

The power of plants
as healers, with planting
guides and remedies for the
mind, body and soul.

70

Publishing Director
Alison Goff
Creative Director
Keith Martin
Executive Editor
Julian Brown
Executive Art Editor
Mark Winwood
Editor
Karen O'Grady
Production Controller
Sarah Scanlon
Picture Research
Joanne Beardwell

First published in Great Britain in 2000 by Hamlyn, a division of Octopus Publishing Group Limited 2-4 Heron Quays, London E14 4JB

Distributed in the United States and Canada by Sterling Publishing Co., Inc 387 Park Avenue South New York, NY 10016 - 8810

A catalogue record for this book is available from the British Library

Produced by Toppan
Printed in China

learning to speak earth's language

a celebration of nature in the garden

Let us suppose for a moment that the earth is a sentient being, capable in her own mysterious way, of intelligent action, of adaptation and skillful manoeuvring to preserve and defend her life giving mission. And again, let's imagine that in moments of insight and true inspiration we might learn to speak her language, to communicate and even assist in that mission. . .

What you now hold in your hands you may have found in the gardening section of your local bookstore, but this book is not at all like other gardening books. Whilst you will find practical tasks, design ideas and exercises, this is not a manual, it will not tell you how to plant an herbaceous border or show you techniques for heeling-in a shrubbery. In contrast, here is a celebration of the art and inspiration of Nature – the harmonious integration of form, line, texture, colour and pattern, as they have been brought together in gardens specifically designed to lift the spirit, stimulate the senses and provide a sanctuary in which to contemplate the deepest meaning of life.

from *essential to sacred*

From the ancient Egyptians, throughout Persia and the Mughal empires, from the Tao in the east to the western renaissance, the lands surrounding our houses, have served as a retreat, a haven for quiet contemplation, a place to reclaim order and to evoke pleasure and spiritual regeneration. Take a look back into the history of these gardens and what may have started as a practical necessity to grow foods or medicine has soon taken on a form and design to express the aesthetic, the creative, the sacred.

the sanctuary outside the back door
exploring our relationship with nature

Now, in our post-modern life, so characterised by artificiality, separateness and the suppression of nature, we are once again developing a deep need for spiritual uplift. Movement and urbanisation have created spiritual introverts. We are losing our sense of proportion, our sense of the fitness of things, rapidly losing our connection with a greater knowing and knowledge that might provide our lives with a meaningful context. Many of us are beginning to believe that it is through such feelings of unease that our own unconscious wisdom is attempting to alert us. The evidence of our own psychology suggests not only that connectedness, peace and clarity are attainable, but that it is the natural and healthy mode of human consciousness. Without it we are simply not whole and, in order to re-connect with our much needed sense of the sacred, we must find ways to create it anew, either internally or, perhaps if that is too great a task for now, in the closest proximity, at home.

We will begin our search for those connections by exploring our deepest relationship with nature. How, for example, we are affected by seasonal variations and how, having once understood these rhythms, we can use them to our benefit. We will investigate the results of those previous cultures who had invested huge economic, physical and artistic resources in creating sacred spaces. We will explore the elements of nature, light and its colours, the sounds, the aromas, textures and shapes. We will describe our aesthetic and psychological responses, the archetypal symbols and long held insights which are deeply precious to us and inseparably bound up with our whole understanding of life. We will explain and seek to understand how it is that in the midst of our now highly unnatural lives, nature still holds the key to magic and mystery, to the enduring questions of who we are, where do we come from and what is the meaning of our lives...

And, there is perhaps an even more urgent purpose. As we continue to diverge from the way we were designed to function, nature is sending us more and more warning signals...

The death of thousands of lakes and forests from the effects of acid rain, the thinning of the ozone layer creating epidemics of skin cancer, and a greenhouse effect, driven by carbon dioxide released from the burning of fossil fuels, that is changing our global weather patterns. And more; the disappearance of tens of thousands of species as a result of the clear-cutting of rain forest and, the loss of millions of tons of irreplaceable top-soil due to modern mechanised agricultural practice. These and other warning signals all portend apocalyptic catastrophes that can only be averted if we take immediate steps to change our fundamental relationship with the natural environment.

Create Your Own Sacred Garden

If we are to create a Garden Sanctuary for today, we will surely want to take into account our new environmental concerns, including the need to husband precious natural resources, to preserve and encourage wildlife, and to make use of our reawakened knowledge of the many factors that can affect not only our health and well being, but also that of the planet. By bringing together all of the elements we will have discovered, as both a personal and global therapy in celebration of nature, we will design and create our own Garden Sanctuary. You are invited to follow and create an inspirational sanctuary for yourself. A personal garden for your own healing, change and daily regeneration.

seasonal gardens

The garden as a metaphor

Every gardener knows the benefits of understanding the cycles and rhythms of the seasons, but there are deeper meanings beyond the climatic and the sun's declination. Look at your garden and the seasonal changes in nature around you. As the seasons pass you will see changes that act as a metaphor for your own life. The seed is the beginning; our own birth and flowering which gains momentum as the essential development of our character takes place, through to the propagation of our own seed. As the garden matures, so do we, until our decay when it becomes the turn of the next generation.

The purpose for considering our garden in any way other than simply as a practical endeavour is that it may give us feedback in the search for our own potential, as well as improving our enjoyment of life as we understand its processes.

Over the years the collective passion for growing food and flowers has probably been the single most important factor in our everyday understanding of nature and how it works. We know we have to work with, not against nature, so when thinking about creating a garden sanctuary, it is crucial to develop a deeper understanding of the natural world. When expressing a modern idea of the sacred, we need to reflect not only on the symbols and experience of the past, but also on our greater understanding and concerns for the natural environment. We start our creation of a garden sanctuary by exploring the many traditions and activities associated with the seasons.

the natural calendar

The natural calendar is depicted here as an eight-spoked wheel, representing our annual seasonal cycle – a progression of nature's events. Each of the 'cardinal points' or quarter days of the year shows the important moments of change; the intervals are shown each with their compass points, their associated colours, elements, the atmosphere they create, and parts of the human body that are believed to be ruled by that season. If you superimposed the wheel over a plan of your garden, you would see the kinds of objects to be placed in each area for particular harmony, and the kind of feeling or atmosphere that might be invoked in these.

' When the positive growth energy has reached its highest point, the negative or decaying force begins to rise, and when this has reached its greatest altitude it also begins to decline. When the moon has waxed to its full it begins to wane. This is the changeless Wheel of Life. When forces have reached their climax, they begin to weaken and when natural things have become fully agglomerated they begin to disperse. After the year's fullness follows decay, and the keenest joy is followed by sadness. This too is the changeless condition of humankind.'

Liu Tzu, around 550BC

The procession of festivals

A great circle is divided into four: north, south, east and west. The circle is then divided again across the diagonal so it cuts the circle north west to south east, and north east to south west. This is the 'Wheel of the Year'. The wheel is further divided into two parts to represent a dark and light half of the year.

The dark half starts in the earth's northern hemisphere on November 1st (north west), the day of the festival of Samhain, or Halloween, and ends on May 1st, the day of the festival of Beltane or May Day (south east). It passes through the darkness and 'death' of winter and, after the festival of Imbolc or Candlemass (north east), is 'reborn' in spring.

The light half of the year takes us through the heat of summer and, after the festival of Lugnasadh or Lammas (south west), enters autumn, the time of harvest. As the days shorten and the light begins to fade, the seeds, having ripened, fall to the ground, once again to be held and transformed by the magic of winter. These are known as 'Lunar' festivals and they mark the passing of the last and the coming of the next part of the cycle.

Imbolc or **Candlemass** marks the passing of winter and the coming of spring, a time of purification and preparation.
Beltane or **May Day** brings fertility and fecundity. It marks the end of spring and the coming of summer.
Lugnasadh or **Lammas** gives thanks for the first harvest of corn and the impending harvests of berries and fruit and celebrates the passing of summer and the coming of autumn.
Samhain or **Halloween** marks the end of autumn. It anticipates the coming darkness, celebrating the approach of winter.
The 'solar' festivals, mid-winter and mid-summer (north and south) are called 'solstices' and the spring and autumn mid-points (east and west) are the 'equinoxes'.

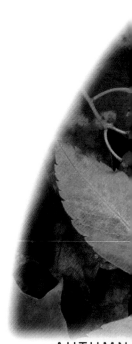

AUTUMN

WINTER SOLSTICE

SAMHAIN/HALLOWEEN

IMBOLC/CANDLEMASS

EQUINOX

SPRING EQUINOX

LUGNASADH/LAMMAS

SUMMER SOLSTICE

BELTANE/MAY DAY

N
W · E
S

Association of elements in the procession of festivals

Association of colours in the procession of festivals

Association of emotions in the procession of festivals

'When the great earth, abandoning day, rolls up the deeps of the heavens and the universe, a new door opens for the human spirit… For a moment of night we have a glimpse of ourselves and of our world islanded in its stream of stars…'

Henry Beston –
American writer and naturalist

Association of garden objects in the
procession of festivals

Association of movement in the
procession of festivals

Association of parts of the body in the
procession of festivals

In the following pages we
will look at each season,
exploring its implications,
personal meaning and
traditional celebrations.
Through appropriate tasks
in the garden, witnessing
wildlife activity and seasonal
meditation exercises, we may
direct our energies and expec-
tations to complement and
coincide with each season.

winter

– the sense of incompleteness

In Japan they have an idea called **fusoki-shugi.** It means the aesthetic, or art in the imagination, of incompleteness. It is the beauty of what has been left out, of what is no more and what is yet to come. It takes on a particular meaning in our northern climes where winter is quite starkly the end, and the beginning of everything.

In the garden, we have cleaned and fertilised the soil, pruned the tired growth, exhausted after the year's energy explosion. And now we wait. Wait, knowing that the magic of death and rebirth is happening unseen.

Amidst the abundance of summer and autumn any garden can look good, but it is in the pallor of winter that you can see the foundation structure. See its beauty and, in so seeing, nurture it now, and the rest will follow.

meditation technique

Don't believe anyone who tells you that meditation is difficult or some secret art. It isn't. If you follow a few simple rules and make it a pleasure, you will benefit from it. Here is a technique to help. For all of the meditations that follow, sit in your favourite place in the garden, close your eyes and go inside. Begin by counting your breathing. Count to ten while you breathe in completely. Hold your breath for the count of seven. Then take 12 seconds to breathe out completely. Hold for another seven seconds and begin again. Practice this at any time. Make sure that your chest is wide open and that you are sitting or lying comfortably. The aim is for you to relax and forget all other thoughts. If you keep thinking about other things, don't worry, just calmly bring yourself back to the counting and carry on.

Winter meditation

For your winter meditation, sit in your favourite place in the garden; wrap up warm! Begin by counting your breathing; relax and close your eyes. Specifically for the winter months, once you are relaxed, start to introduce the following thoughts. . .

The act of creation is pure magic. It is joyful, impossible and yet it happens: a most primitive and powerful force. Always, if the foundation work is genuine, the final form will be appropriate to the need and every element of it will belong to the whole, to everything else that is going on.

For the moment, explore the concept of 'appropriate form'. Just like making up case studies, think of creations in the garden that worked, either those of your own or of some acknowledged expert.

In the garden, what were last year's successes and failures? Do you know why? What was not appropriate or 'out of place' about the foundations of the failures? Conversely, what was appropriate about the foundations of the successes? Did they meet a real need that was an answer for other things in the garden? Can you identify them? For example, perhaps you had decided to introduce stone or pebbles. If the garden was dry and these stones held the water, grew moss or enhanced the colours, then they did answer some other question or need. You don't have to look for complicated things; it might be something very simple. One can develop an aesthetic 'feel' for the appropriateness of these creations, helped by this exercise.

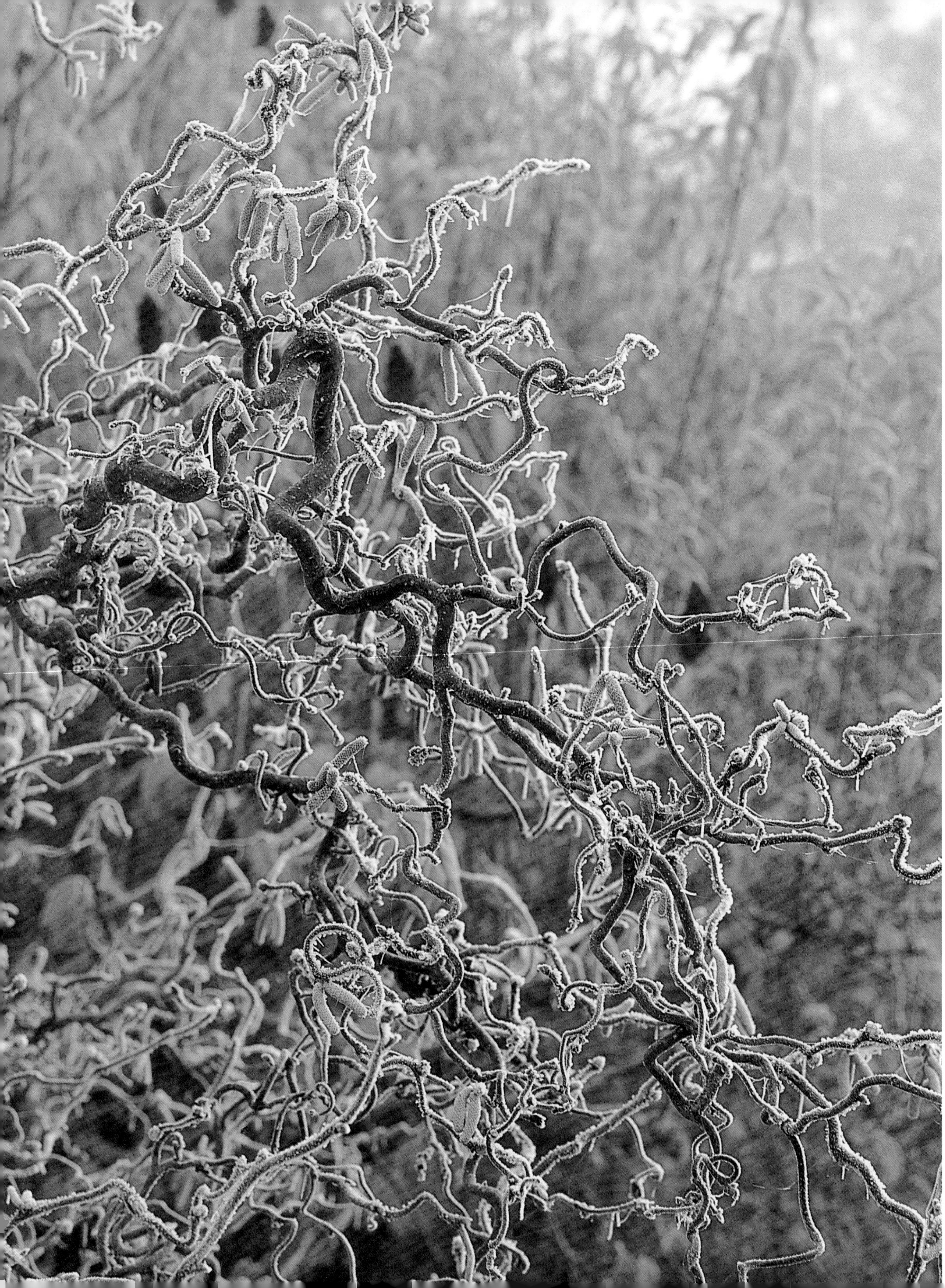

Winter begins at **Samhain**, or **Halloween**, the feast of autumn's end. This day marks the end of the harvest and the close of the year's light half, when it is exactly an eighth of the year until the shortest day. Halloween, is also the Celtic New Year, a night existing 'between the worlds', when it is said that a crack in time opens our subconscious to seek visions and inspiration for the coming period of inner contemplation.

For your celebrations, invite friends, light a fire and candles in the garden, sit around the fire and tell the stories of your memories. A symbolic meal for the season will include as many of this year's harvested crops as possible. After the supper, play games that honour the harvest fruit, like apple-bobbing or biting an apple on a string.

In winter, all is dormant like the age-old yew that seems hardly to move. Growing so slowly, it is the embodiment of death and continuing life, immortality in stillness.

The winter solstice is the time of the shortest days and longest nights. All growth is stopped by the powerful transforming darkness. Mysterious, renewing from within its protection, the spark of new life is born. From now on, as the days begin to draw out, the spark will begin to glow in the dark. As a symbolic ceremony, sit in your winter place in the garden by the water. Keep a flame alive all night and wait until the dawn.

Christmas brings light and new hope to the world, the Mother bears the divine Child. Sing and dance to carols. We always decorate trees, but any plant in the garden will do. Hang bells, gold and silver streamers to reflect and increase the light, and crown with a star to reach out to.

Imbolc, **Candlemass** or **St Brigit's Day** is the festival of fertility and growing light. The light is seeking, renewing and rejuvenating. Creative energy is rising. The traditional unwinding spiral dance empowers the creative urge that is not yet formed. A meal including the remains from last year's harvest is cooked in new pots and offered, as you eat, to the waxing sun.

winter *wildlife garden*

At this time of year the garden literally becomes a sanctuary for foraging birds. Native and resident species return to their over-winter homes and, although the hedgerows are often still full of fruiting hips and berries, it is time to begin winter feeding. Native mammals are still active in the woods and hedgerows; they may visit the garden after dark.

Frozen it may be, but beneath the surface the garden is still teeming with life. Don't clear up too much. Leave some flower-beds to die back naturally. Piles of leaves and debris will shelter spiders, insects and even smaller mammals. Choose a quiet corner to a winter home for insects, reptiles and mammals using a wood or rock.

winter *garden tasks*

Make a leaf mould from the abundance of autumn leaves with a wire-netting cylinder attached to a stake. Firm down and water. After one year you will have created leaf-mould compost or mulch. Plant spring-flowering bulbs. Remember the compost heap! Having emptied or turned it during the autumn, begin rebuilding. It will continue to generate heat during the winter, and so is a good place to plant some seeds for early germination. No matter how small, it is quite literally the best example in the garden of new life from old. When conditions permit this is a good time to move, replant and feed trees and plants, roses and shrubs. Protect non-hardy plants and continue your pruning of old, dead and damaged growth. All sowing and growing must take place indoors or under cover. Only digging, manuring and preparing the ground is recommended for outside.

spring
– the energising spirit of nature

The energising spirit of nature in spring, is probably the strongest metaphor for our deepest relationship with the natural world, inspiring transition and change. Spring contains all of the latent force of the previous year, inexorably changing and building within the germinating seed. As the new life begins to emerge, nature displays its victory once again. As the days grow longer and slowly warmer, the first flush of yellow flowers acts like a beacon to the emerging insects. We too react to the light and, with renewed fervour, come to look on the world with new eyes, after the dark and inward contemplation of winter.

How often it is said that love blossoms in the spring. Our horizons begin to expand and we want to be outside more, to move, to travel, to explore and build beyond our insular world.

'We had the sky up there, all speckled with stars, and we used to lay on our backs and look up at them, and discuss about whether they was made, or only just happened.'

Mark Twain

Spring meditation

Look back to the meditation technique on page 16. Start by sitting in your favourite place in the garden. Begin your breathing, relax and when you are ready, consider these thoughts.

There are now special and practical tasks to be done: sowing, planting and propagating for the year ahead. We need to feel free and motivated in our intention to work, to be assured of our own capability and commitment. So, think of a time in the future when all your creative capabilities will be available to you to use in your work.

Ask yourself, if I could have whatever I wish for, what would I be able to do that I cannot do at this present time? What do I want to achieve? Let your imagination run free. Think of yourself at your best. What does it feel like to have achieved so much? What will it mean to you and to others? If you need to, write the ideas down on paper. For now, don't worry about how all this will happen.

As you do this exercise, a vision of the future will begin to grow. In your imagination, concentrate simply on the details of this future form, and don't hold back! Go so far as to imagine the kind of butterfly that will emerge from the chrysalis of your present. Don't be afraid to feel what it would be like to fly.

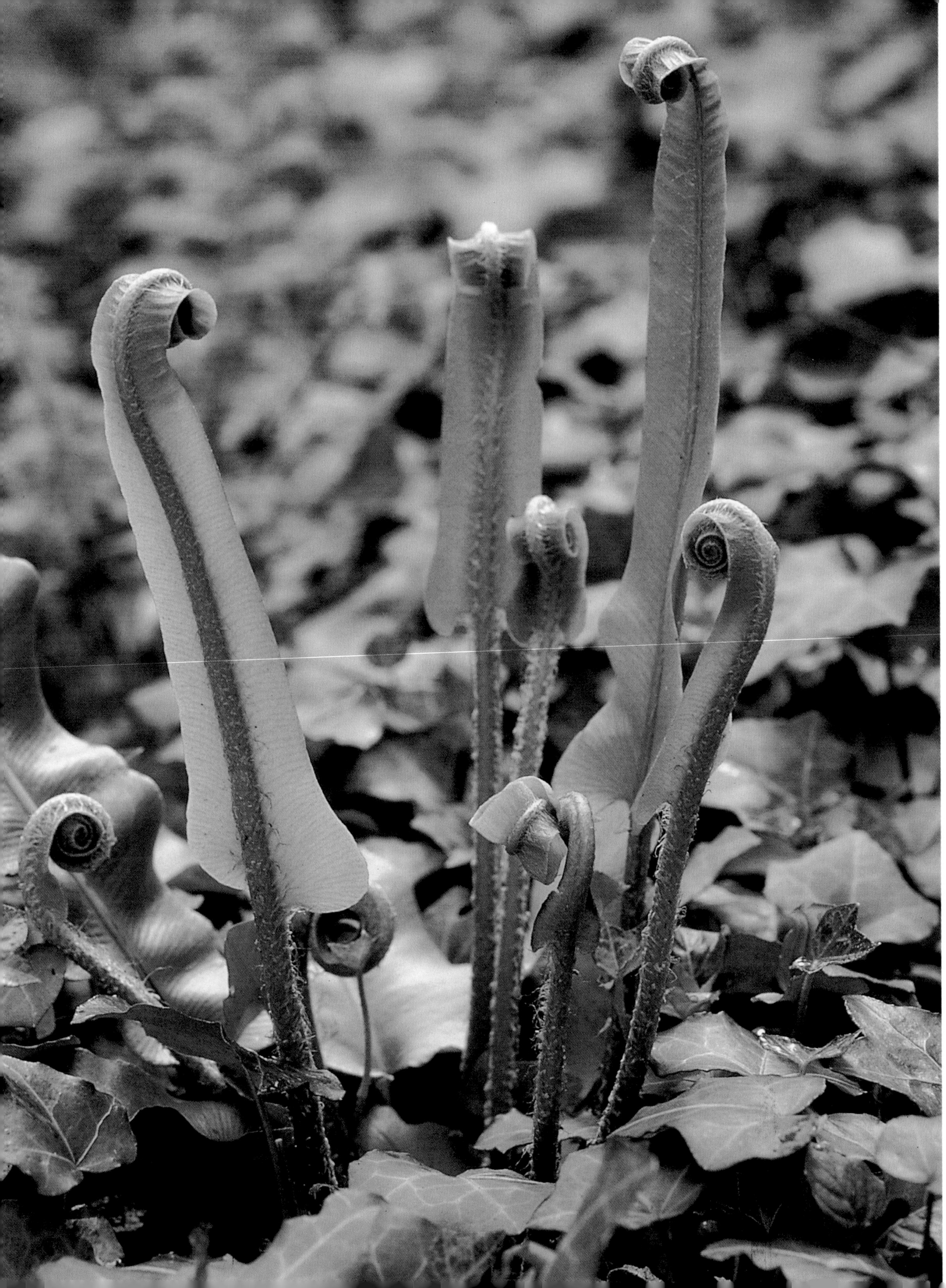

spring *traditions and activities*

At the **spring equinox** the sun crosses the equator. The god of the land having died, is reborn and, rising again with out-bursts of light and joy, is reunited with the goddess, his lover. It is a very old tradition in many belief systems around the world, that fasting and cleansing should end now, marked at this precise moment of change with feasting and prayers for the coming fertility. Many games and ceremonies have been devised as metaphors for this important moment and, many symbols like eggs and more recently, rabbits, are used to portray the seed and fecundity of the life to come.

Growing in wet places, the alder seeds float downstream to start new groves.

A most important quarter day, **Beltane** or **May Day** heralds the end of spring and the coming of summer. This is the real beginning of the light half of the year and one of the most celebrated throughout time.

Encouraged with bouquets of spring flowers, visions of youth and sex, the **Celtic Goddess of May Eve**, **Queen Mab of the Fairies**, awakes. The tradition calls for a fire to be lit and danced around at sunrise. It is customary to leap three times over the flames. Eat cakes made at the Full Moon and drink wine or cider from last year's harvest. Say a prayer over special water and silently wash or drink. Bring in the summer in the early morning by decorating the garden with May blossom. In the evening, dance around a selected plant, tree or stone symbolising summer. An ancient tale suggests that if you run around your house carrying a wand of this month's tree symbol, the willow, you will see your future lover grasping the other end of the stick.

spring *wildlife garden*

During the very beginning of spring the days lengthen and the early morning chorus becomes a little more lively. The male bird population announces its interest in a mate. Even in a small town garden, if the conditions are there, you will almost certainly have one nesting pair. Feeding is still important, whatever the weather, as this is a vital time for building up strength. If it's mild, frogs and toads begin to emerge. Butterflies may be stirred into life by a spell of weak sunshine. The hazel and the alder become active in hanging their catkins and, at ground level, a growing carpet of bulbs, celandines and violets emerges, offering waking food for insects. Available nest-building material encourages birds to use your garden. That slightly unkempt flower bed or compost heap now flourishes. In the wild, the onset of spring is often signalled by a flush of bright flowers, and while frosts and snow flurries may interrupt the birth, the inexorable energy of new life can only be slowed. As the season expands, summer migrants begin to arrive and mammals born underground slowly open their eyes and gather strength to move around.

spring *garden tasks*

It is the season for planting, preparing and feeding planting sites. This alternative time for pruning now adds root pruning and coppicing for both new growth and to encourage flowering. Re-potting and sowing under protection gives everything an added advantage when the soil outside warms up enough to begin planting. Fertilise and mulch for the new growth. As soon as conditions permit, start planting out, dividing and replanting perennials and container-grown plants. Protect early fruit flowers from the cold and erect supports for climbers. It is time to initiate any new projects planned over the winter months.

summer
– the triumph of light over dark

The pace quickens, the ecstatic culmination of the sun, the triumph of light over dark, demands that every manifestation of life takes this opportunity to flower, to bear fruit and to absorb the nourishment provided, stretching the life-force to the limit and expressing creativity in return. **'Make hay while the sun shines'** is not just a neat adage but an urgent supplication. Amid fullness and clamour, the unfaltering strength of purpose and colour at its climax, nature's all powerful demand to flower and set seed ensures the very continuity of life itself. If abundance is the keynote of summer, then purification is the essential task to ensure a clean and healthy harvest. The sun is warm; it is the fire season of bursting joy. Everything is open, full-on, sometimes heady and overpowering in the hot and humid air.

To prepare the agnihotre

Here are some things you will have to prepare for the Agnihotre , 'the purified atmosphere'. The Hindu Vedic tradition uses an upturned ziggurat or metal bowl in which to light the little fire. Collect small, very dry tinder sticks. They will burn fast so make sure you have plenty. You want the strongest mini-flame you can manage in which to burn dried Marigold or St John's Wort/Hypericum petals. These are particularly symbolic of gold, sun and light, but any flower will do. When the flame is hot you might also burn herbs, some dried sage perhaps, or some special seeds that you saved from last year's harvest.

Call and sing out any words that you think might be appropriate to describe your desire to clean the atmosphere.

Summer meditation – the agnihotre

For our summer meditation, sit in your favourite place in the garden. Try the south quarter, close your eyes and go inside yourself. Begin your breathing count and when you are feeling relaxed, introduce this thought.

The act of creation produces such dramatic changes in the world. Everything can be affected: nature, objects, customs, attitudes. There is a lot of clamour and things can get confused in the melee and the profusion of bursting life. Cleaning is the key to ensuring the purity of the result – creating a healthy space for growth. In the garden, this means weeding, clearing, making a healthy and productive growing environment.

The cycle of growth, from being conceived and being born to flowering, fruiting and maturity, is a phenomenon of metamorphosis. For such a change to occur externally, it must be preceded by a change in the creator's inner world. In the meditations for winter and spring we prepared the ground; stillness and contemplation were followed by gathering motivation and strength. Now we look to a metamorphosis in ourselves to provide a new level of creative insight and expression. We will bring about that metamorphosis symbolically, as the flame does to the atmosphere, by purification with a little fire ceremony at the end of the meditation.

Meanwhile, think about all the changes that have occurred in the garden from winter through spring and summer. Think about the factors that both promote and prevent this metamorphosis; those that delay or hamper its occurrence. It can be subtle. Consider the effect that pollution must be having on the growth of our food and its release of nutrients to us. As you promote a positive outcome in the garden by weeding, cleaning, feeding and watering, do so in your meditation. Visualise a single cleansing flame, burning bright, strong, upright and full, by its very nature transforming the subtle air it contacts.

Purify the atmosphere with sacred flame – the agnihotre ceremony

There is a Hindu Vedic technique called *Vajna*, which refers to the purifying effect of fire on the atmosphere. Nothing is destroyed, only changed by the fire. 'Nutrients are injected into the atmosphere' and the sun's rays are thereby better absorbed. 'Plants grown in the Agnihotre or purified atmosphere, create a healing effect on body and mind.'

After spending a short time thinking about this, you may like to follow the old tradition that exists in many cultures, of actually lighting a small but symbolic flame to clean the atmosphere.

summer *traditions and activities*

Early in the season at the full moon after **Beltane**, it is time to celebrate **Wesak,** the birthday of the **Buddha**. A truly summer-like celebration of enlightenment and passing into paradise or **Nirvana**, in recent years the festival has represented the coming together of all religions. The tradition is to light the home and garden with paper lanterns, to water special trees and plants and to walk in the lamplit garden in the evening.

Hawthorn, the tree of hope, is an early sign of summer. Sprigs and branches gathered from the greenwood, are carried from door to door and placed in the middle of the floor around which to dance.

The summer solstice, when the sun is at its zenith, resulting in the longest day and shortest night, is a peak moment of promise. The wheel of the year descends, and fire again is the traditional emblem for encouraging the light: Try lighting hilltop bonfires, processing with lamps, rolling flaming wheels, and keeping a flame alive until dawn; when ritual bathing greets the sun.

The season of outdoor parties and eating outside, outdoor fêtes and festivities are traditional throughout the world.

Groves of oak were once used for worship, the great bows pollarded and trained to mount platforms for feasting and dancing in the trees. A tradition in many cultures at mid-summer eve is to decorate trees and plants with paper messages or prayer flags. The colourful wishes of good luck are transported on the warm summer air.

Now is when most of the garden wildlife bring up their young, feeding, protecting, running back and forth. Resident birds start their second brood. Tadpoles emerge to run the gauntlet of predator beetles and mammals. Food supplies are at their most plentiful, slugs and beetles, nectar, and water while it lasts. Young hedgehogs and smaller mammals such as foxes and badgers appear. Bats, fluttering and swooping around the house at twilight, foray for their single young. Dragonflies and damselflies may be seen under the shady hedgerows darting and flashing at smaller insects.

As the season progresses, flowers everywhere reach their peak. Their nectar keeps a myriad of butterflies, bees, caterpillars, moths, hoverflies and ladybirds happy and busy. Fledglings can be seen fluttering around the trees on their maiden flights, with mother in tow, panicking constantly and disturbing every other creature skulking low in the undergrowth, under-going their summer moult. It can be hot in the day with little birdsong or apparent activity. But mornings, for the wake-up, and evenings when all the night scents are at their peak, can be the most rewarding for wildlife watching. Native plants are more resilient to dry spells or changing conditions, but, whatever the weather, nature in every form is at its most vibrant.

summer *garden tasks*

Maintaining a healthy growing space means feeding, watering, weeding and mulching. Early crops and displays need harvesting and cleaning, and tender plants need to be put out. The tasks of pinching out, thinning, supporting and pruning dead wood, dead-heading and picking fruit are each a part of 'cleaning' and making a healthy growing environment.

The colours are clear and the foliage is at its best in the garden. In the meadows, the wild coun-terparts of our arranged beds, the flowers reach their peak, the grass seed is setting and the fruits are well established. The work carried out in winter and spring affords more time to relax and enjoy the fruit and flowers of the labour.

As the season progresses, harvesting begins. It is time to start drying herbs and flowers and of course, eating.

autumn

– energy to fruition

Almost a season in its own right, late summer – **Lammas-tide** is in fact a combination of the seasons. It is the season at the centre, the last ten days of each season, rolled into one'. Amid great changes, a good 'grounding' or connection to the earth is vital.

Quiet strength, the solidity of who we are is determined by our stability on the earth. Operating from within, the earth's order and harmony build the inner mineral resources needed, a scaffolding to make the autumn metal and support for the heavy matured fruit to be harvested. There is nothing unwanted now in our garden sanctuary, no dead wood, no disease, only the sensual sweet flavours of the fruit, the ultimate manifestation of the creative urge. Nature is at her most successful and the most nutritious bounty on earth contains the seed of the next generation.

The days and nights are of equal length now, the force of darkness is increasing but there is great comfort in the bounty: gathering, preserving, bringing home the harvest late into the evening sunset, filling the food store ready for winter.

'There once was a sailor that we all knew
Who had so many things which he wanted to do.
But whenever he thought it was time to begin,
He couldn't because of the state he was in.'

A.A.Milne

Autumn meditation

Look back to the meditation technique on page 16. We would all like to approach our lives with more creative spontaneity. But even if we become calmer and self-assured, we are likely to still need a more deliberate way of gaining clearer insights.

When talking about solving problems, the lateral thinking man, Edward de Bono, invented the idea of Po. It is neither Yes nor No, but waiting, suspending judgement and gathering more information. This involves brain-storming some less usual angles, and trying not to get sidetracked or be biased by old judgements. In letting go of the all-consuming need to solve everything immediately, a little space is created for something new to enter.

Imagine that you are blowing up a huge balloon. Each breath into it represents a single ingredient of a plan or idea that you want to achieve. Perhaps they are the ingredients for the perfect garden. Keep blowing. For now you do not need to concern yourself too much as to how the connections will be made between these, perhaps disparate 'breath-wishes'. As you continue, make a list of the ingredients in your balloon, and say why each of them hold so much meaning for you.

Don't stop at one balloon. Try another with a different subject or a problem. You may end up carrying several 'balloons' around with you at one time and as they become bigger, you'll discover that they have enormous potential to 'lift off' and carry you!

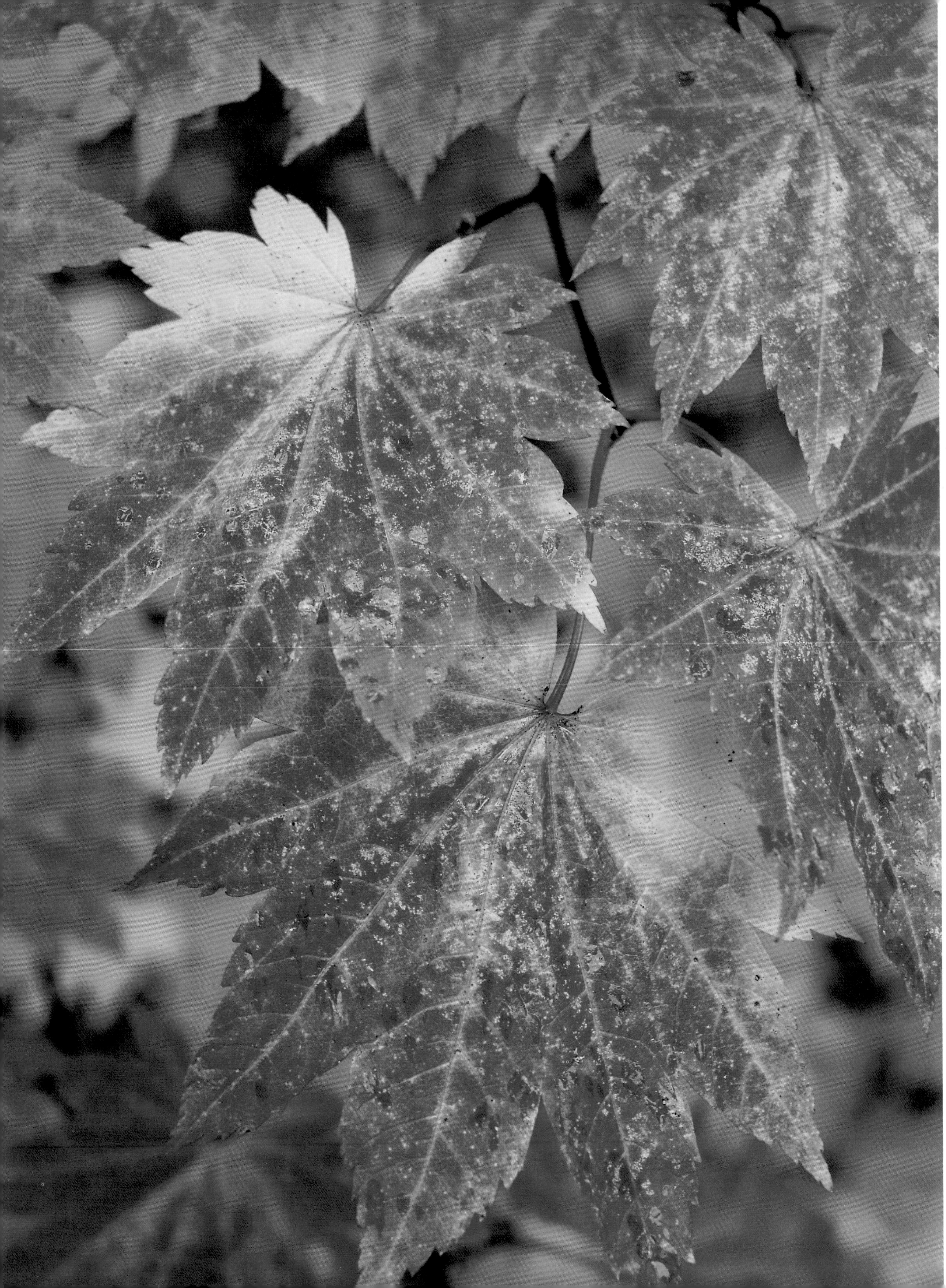

Lammas or **Lugnasadh** marks the beginning of the harvest, the change between flowering and fruiting. The feast of the 'grain goddess', Demeter, is at the first harvest of corn; the harvests of fruit and berries follow. Many traditions, in the 'month of the lightning moon', while celebrating the bounty, also concern the weather and deflect storms until the harvest is in. Once again the symbolic act of keeping alive the light is popular, especially since it is now beginning to wane. Lammas is traditionally also the time for 'rites of passage': making pilgrimages, walking into mazes or labyrinths to symbolise change in oneself. Inbound, the present and past character dies, returning as the 'new' you on your exit from the centre, born again and strengthened by the experience. A special meal prepared with grains such as wheat or barley and summer vegetables, eaten with friends, outside in the garden, is a fitting celebration.

Nakedness Day at Lammas sees Lady Godiva, astride her horse, pursuing the corn king and latterly, supporting the local people's fight against high taxes.

As the nuts begin to swell, Hazel is the symbol of concentrated wisdom. Sea captains wore a sprig as protection against bad weather. This fast-growing species has found many uses, including fences, baskets, thatching spars and building stakes. It is said that although the tree will die within 40 years, a coppiced hazel will last for approximately 1,000 years.

The **Apple**, as a symbol of desire and the consummation of love, appears in many cultures. The crab apple was heavily cultivated throughout Europe for use in wines and tart jellies. Its larger cousins appeared in the history of the Near East more than 4,000 years ago. Love stories, hand-written on paper strips and hung in the apple branches, are said to bring favour.

The climax of **harvest**, with fruit and berries joining the store of grain, is at the **autumn equinox.** Nearing the end of the light half of the year, the last quarter is the fulfilment of the year's labour. The end of the grape harvest is legendary, with eight-day festivals of drinking and eating. In cooler climes, the bramble and its blackberries symbolise the weariness, ultimate death and grief at the season's end. The young god of the land, Adonis, having died at harvest now faces an uncertain and difficult journey through the depths of winter. Carried through the streets on a silver funeral bed, he is adorned with harvest greenery for food and ornaments to light his passage.

Harvest full moon is a pagan festival, its keynotes being **intuition**, **imagination** and **magic**. Often described as the most potent of the year, this full moon is heralded as symbolic of the rhythm of life between heaven and earth.

autumn *wildlife garden*

Early autumn is the best time for wildlife watching as the weather is warm and almost wherever you look there is activity. Most obvious are the insects as any lights or still air will bring them in profusion. The food chain is often quite plain to see, with midge like insects feeding hoverflies, ladybirds and dragonflies. Almost any water at this time of year will attract birds, hedgehogs and foxes, who may forget their timidity for a drink. Birds though are still not much in evidence, their summer moult makes flying difficult and, this is after all, their recovery time from a frenetic year. Some may be leaving soon and will prepare for a burst of activity to announce their departure. The warblers and flycatchers will be the first to move.

As the season progresses, the hedgerows fill with fruit, hips and berries, damsons and hazelnuts. Moths and insects, birds and small mammals are all regularly in attendance. Misty mornings and warm afternoons see nature's own harvest reaching a climax. There is more food available now than at any time in the year and, at every level creatures are gathering strength and stores for the journey to winter homes or the cold months ahead. The meadow and wild plants begin to die back and, late in the season, a first frost will close the year for many.

autumn *garden tasks*

The busiest time of the year in the garden. More work now means less later. On with the harvesting of herbaceous leaves, roots, seeds and fruits. From mid-autumn it is time to lift plants for forcing, sow and plant hardy new and overwintering stocks, tree and shrub seeds. Take hardwood and semi-ripe cuttings to plant in a small prepared trench. Look for vigorous stems just completing their seasons growth. Plant or prune evergreens, repot and top-dress containers and their plants. Do all of the digging, fertilising and mulching now. The frost and the winter passage will break it down and all of the organic material will have been absorbed into rich soil by the time it is needed for spring planting. After mid-autumn, begin to reduce watering. Prune and renovate deciduous shrubs and also trees, training them to your desired shape. Time to plant out the herb garden, plan and prepare plots and borders for next year's arrangement. Plant spring flowering bulbs and don't forget the garlic; in containers or prepared ground. Plant soft fruits for next year, including strawberries.

Autumn is also the best time to collect native tree and plant seeds and berries for propagation. It may be a slow and sometimes erratic process, but it's very rewarding when they sprout and many native species can be grown in this way. Finally, if you have an area of low fertility, this is the time to consider seeding a wildflower and meadow grasses lawn.

feed the senses

Colours, aromas and sounds affect our health

Why we choose particular colours or aromas, in our garden flowers or even the colours of walls or features in the garden, is often a mystery. Do we just like those colours and perfumes, or might there be a deeper reason? We are beginning to understand that there may be substance to the idea that when we have a passion for a particular food or taste, it may be because our internal mechanisms are trying to tell us that we will benefit from the nutrients, vitamins or minerals contained within that food. Similarly, sounds in nature are very important to us. Everyone recognises the pleasure of sitting beside a babbling brook or the sound of wind in the leaves of a tree, or of birdsong.

Modern scientific research shows that these sounds, colours and aromas each have a unique frequency or vibration which, when entering our brains, affects us emotionally, mentally and even physiologically. With this is mind, we may begin to pro-actively choose for our garden those colours, aromas and sounds that will positively enhance our health and attitudes.

colour – more than meets the eye

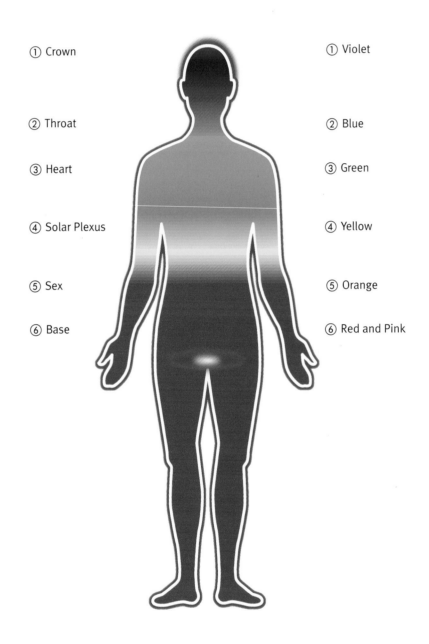

① Crown

② Throat

③ Heart

④ Solar Plexus

⑤ Sex

⑥ Base

① Violet

② Blue

③ Green

④ Yellow

⑤ Orange

⑥ Red and Pink

Much of our behaviour, including our response to colour, is determined by powerful influences and reactions of which we are largely unconscious. When planting for effect in the garden, which colours and colour combinations hold universal appeal or implications for our health and well-being?

When light strikes the eye, each wavelength does so slightly differently: red, the longest, appears nearer and stronger; green requires least adjustment and is therefore restful. The retina converts these vibrations of light into electrical impulses which pass to the brain. Eventually they reach the hypothalamus, governing the endocrine glands, and these, in turn produce and secretes hormones. Simply, each colour wavelength, within a matter of seconds after receiving it, evokes a chemical and physiological response, which then produces a variety of psychological and physical reactions.

Colour therapists believe that parts of the body are ruled by and vibrate to the same frequencies as certain colours. From the base of the body, rising from the feet to red and pink, moving through orange around the belly to yellow at the solar plexus. The area around the heart and chest is green and around the throat light blue. Blue darkens to a royal or deep blue at the forehead and rises to violet at the crown.

close *your eyes and imagine in colour*

Have you ever closed your eyes and seen a myriad of different colours? Because we see and process colour through our eyes, we often imagine that it is simply a matter of appearance. The chemical, then hormonal and psychological reaction, however, shows us that colour is also about feelings. We dream in colour, visualise and imagine in colour, without actually seeing any at all!

As a wavelength, colour is a specific vibration of energy, like a musical note. It is around us and, perhaps more importantly, in us, all the time. Kirlian photography has shown that there is an aura of colour surrounding each one of us, in which colours change as our mental, emotional and physical health changes. The whole idea of nature is enhanced when we realise that these colours consist only of atmospheric particles of energy or photons, which when they strike an object are absorbed or reflected depending on the structure of that object. The object will absorb only those wavelengths and particles of light, which exactly match its own atomic structure. The rest is reflected back as the colour that we see. We may feel that we like a certain colour, or have a certain affinity for a colour and, in many medicinal practices around the world, the practitioner will take this as a key to our health. Perhaps we too absorb the colours that suit our state of health or distress and reflect those which do not match it. It would follow then, that the colours we choose to have around us, in the garden for example, those particles of light that we allow or encourage into our lives, are likely to have an enormous effect on our health and well-being.

The following pages offer a consensus of ideas, ancient and modern, about the effects of colour on our health and attitudes, and as plant combinations to produce those colours in the flower border or as bolder features. Plants known to embody symbolic or healing character have been included. It should also be noted that some plants have an 'essential' or deep colour that is sometimes not reflected in its flowers or foliage. This may be the colour of the oil or a chemical produced.

It is important to remember that although many of the plants mentioned have a medicinal use, this often requires an expert knowledge of medicinal remedies. Therefore, we strongly recommend that you consult with a qualified practitioner of herbal or homeopathic medicine before you use them.

red and pink

Red is the warming, energising energy or wavelength colour in nature. Red brings with it physical strength, stamina and vitality. Red helps us when we are tired, listless or depressed. It promotes heat in the body, helping the circulation and the production of healthy red blood cells. In traditional Chinese medicine it is the colour of joy, of excitement and sensual, sexual love. It gives purpose and strengthens our will to take action, and also helps to keep us grounded.

Pink is the quieter, gentler, more feminine aspect of red. It softly warms and, more subtly, energises, making it especially useful for the young, the old or weak. Consisting of red light mixed with white, it is comforting and uplifting in a calmer way than the one-pointed, forcefulness of red. While red is masculine in its quality, it is about basic material survival; fight or flight. Pink is more feminine, nurturing that survival, soothing its difficulties.

For a balance there should not be an abundance of any one colour. Pink is warming and nourishing, but it needs green or blue to refresh it.

Before you turn the page to look at the red and pink plant selection, take a moment to look at this page. Close your eyes and let the impression remain with you. Quietly make up your mind about how this colour makes you feel and what thoughts come into your mind.

red and pink

the flowers

Bergamot/*Monarda bradburyana* 'Cambridge Scarlet'
A brilliant herb flower (not the Earl Grey flavouring which is a citron). For coughs, and fevers, anxiety and lack of confidence.
Red – Fully hardy, needing sun and moist soil.

Boston ivy/*Parthenocissus tricuspidata*
Green flowers in summer and the most spectacular crimson leaves in autumn.
Green and Red – Fast-growing, fully to half-hardy, prefers semi-shade or shade in well-drained soil.

Camellia/*Camellia*
The Victorian's flower of perfect loveliness. One of the most beautiful early blooms.
Pink and Red – There are many varieties, fully hardy to frost tender, preferring sheltered, semi-shaded, well-drained, neutral to acid soil.

Campion/*Silene; Lychnis*
The Bladder, Ragged Robin, Red and White Campion. Very pretty hedgerow flowers.
Pink – Fully to half-hardy, needing sun and well-drained soil.

Centaury/*Erythraea centaurium*
In Greek mythology, the Centaur, Chairon used it to heal Hercules. The flowers are gathered and slow dried to make an infusion as an aperitif.
Pink and Red – Fully hardy, it prefers sun and well-drained soil.

Cherry/*Prunus*
The early, evocative spring blossom. It succeeds in so many ways, a beautiful sign of coming spring, vitamin-rich fruits and an early source of nectar for flying insects.
Pink – Fully hardy, preferring sun in any but waterlogged soil.

Clary sage/*Salvia sclarea*
The flower of elation. Its name means clear. It is an excellent tonic for stress related problems. Very similar to sage in its effects and indications.
Red and Pink – Fully hardy to frost tender. Needs sun and well-drained soil.

Comfrey/*Symphytum officinale*
'The knitbone flower'. Best suited to the wild garden where it can spread freely. Culpepper recommends the root for bruises, ruptures and fractures. Seek further advice, as this is a powerful herb.
Pink – Fully hardy, it prefers sun or semi-shade in moist soil.

Coneflower/
Echinacea augustifolia
The flower of wholeness. As an essence it is well known for taking at the first signs of infection, colds, sore throats and flu. It has both anti biotic and anti viral effects.
Pink and Purple – Fully hardy, prefers sun and humus rich, moist but well-drained soil.

Crab apple/*Malus sylvestris*
Endangered species in the wild; the Bach flower essence is for detoxifying and cleansing of wounds, either physical or emotional. The fruits make good pickle or a pectin-rich base for jams. Best for fruit jellies.
Pink and White – A small tree, slow-growing, preferring sun. They will grow in all but waterlogged soil.

Dicentra formosa
The bleeding heart flower. Helps to promote inner peace and strength with the ability to give love.
Red and Pink – Fully hardy perennial, prefers semi-shade and humus-rich, well-drained soil.

Dog rose/*Rosa canina*
The flower of love. Sweet-scented blossoms. An infusion of the petals helps infection, clearing heat and toxins. The hips require care in preparation, but are the most abundant source of plant Vitamin C.
Pink – A wide genus, they are usually fully hardy, in open, sunny, fertile and moist draining soil.

Flowering quince/*Chaenomeles speciosa*
Crimson flowers during winter and spring with fruits used in preserves in the autumn. The flower essence is to make strength.
Red – Fully hardy, they prefer sun and well-drained soil.

Hawthorn/*Crataegus laevigata*
May. Red flowers and berries. A small shrubby tree for wildlife.
Red – Fully hardy, preferring full sun in any but wet soil.

Heather/*Calluna vulgaris*
The Flower of Good Fortune. The Bach flower essence is for lonely people.
Pink – Fully to frost-hardy in open, sunny, humus rich draining soil.

Hibiscus/*Hibiscus rosa-sinensis; H. syriacus* (ornamental varieties)
The flower of love and worship in the East The famous and delicious tea. Helps to connect caring love and sex.
Red – Difficult to grow, and slow. Try in a container so that it can be moved into the sun and protected.

Hollyhock/*Alcea rosa*
Tall spikes of soft flowers. Used for calming digestive, respiratory and urinal complaints. Cools excessive heat.
Red and Pink – Fully hardy, needs full sun and well-drained soil.

Impatiens balfourii
The poor man's orchid. 'Indian Balsam'. The Bach Flower essence is for impatience.
Red and Pink – Can be invasive. Frost hardy, prefers sun or semi-shade, in moist but draining soil.

Japanese maple/*Acer palmatum*
The dying leaves are vivid red.
Red – Fully to frost-hardy, in sun or semi-shade. Best leaf colour when in neutral to acid soil.

Mallow/*Malva*
The flowers of softness. These plants have been used for soothing digestive, respiratory and urinal complaints. A cooling effect on excessive heat or inflammation.
Red and Pink – Natives of saltmarsh and damp, fertile places, they are fully hardy, needing full sun and draining soil.

At the base is red. It's the warming, energising energy or wavelength colour in nature. Pink is the quieter, gentler, more feminine aspect of red.

Mountain pride/*Penstemon newberryi*

The flowers of strength and assertiveness. Deep rose pink flowers in early summer. It is said to be for those who withdraw in the face of a challenge.

Pink – Good for the rock garden. Trim after flowering. Fully to half-hardy, preferring full sun and well-drained soil.

Pennyroyal/*Mentha pulegium*

Related to peppermint and catmint. An endangered species.

Pink and Purple – An herbaceous edging plant, fully to frost-hardy, likes sun or shade in well-drained soil.

Peony/*Paeonia lactiflora; P. officinalis*

The Flowers of Radiance. The name derives from the mystical Paeon, healer of the Gods. In Chinese traditional medicine the root is used for wounds, headaches and poor circulation. The essence is prescribed for those affected by negative influences.

Red and Pink – half-hardy, they prefer sun or light shade in rich, well-drained soil.

Poppy/*Papaver rhoeas*

Corn Poppy, Field Poppy, the flower of blood and new life.

Red – Self-seeding easily in sun and poor well-drained soil.

Red valerian/*Centranthus ruber*

The Valerian family is well know to healers and in sacred rites. *Officinalis* is the species where the root is used as a sedative. Often scented, found among rocks and old walls.

Red to pink – A hardy perennial, preferring sun and a more alkaline, well-drained soil.

Sainfoin/*Onobrychis viciifolia*

'Holy Hay'. A fodder plant from the seventeenth century, now widely naturalised on road embankments.

Pink – Frost hardy tall spears, preferring sun and well-drained soil.

Saxifrage/*Saxifraga oppositifolia; S. x urbinum*

A declining species of old chalk grasslands and damp hay meadows, naturalised in walls and rock banks. Spring flowers for the butterflies and bees.

Pink – Fully to half-hardy, likes shade from the midday sun. Prefers a moist, draining peat soil.

Scarlet pimpernel/*Anargallis arvensis*

'Poor Man's Weatherglass'/'Go to bed at noon'. Flowers close in the afternoon or on dull days.

Red – A half-hardy annual, they prefer full sun and almost any draining soil.

Smoke bush/*Cotinus coggygria*

Flame variety has vivid red autumnal colour.

Red – Fully hardy, prefers sun or semi-shade in not over-rich fertile soil.

Sweet marjoram/ *Origanum marjorana*

The flower of honour. In Greek 'joy of the mountain'. Culinary and medicinal, it helps protect against infection. For digestion it is anti-spasmodic, warming and relaxing.

Pink – Useful for trailing over rocks and banks. Fully to frost-hardy, prefers sun and well-drained soil.

Vervain/*Verbena officinalis*

The flower of divination, the sacred flower of the altar. A tonic for the nervous system, calming tension, relieving anxiety.

Pink and Blue – Frost hardy and growing easily in most well-drained soil, it prefers sun.

Thyme/*Thymus vulgaris*

The flower of bravery. Burned at the altar in ancient Greece. A powerful internal and external antiseptic. Boosts the immune system and good for colds and flu. Good for memory and enhancing concentration. A natural aphrodisiac.

Pink and White – Hugs the ground, can be walked on. Fully to half-hardy in sun and moist, draining soil.

orange and yellow

Orange heats like the reds, but its heat is softened by intellectual, more analytical yellow; It is the colour of opening, like orange traffic lights, it is preparing for movement, and so is more expansive and toning. With orange we develop self-confidence and self-respect. It has a freeing action on many levels. It frees the emotions, allowing their expression, it can be helpful with overcoming creative blocks. Orange opens up movement so that we can be more graceful and flowing and it frees the movement of body fluids, the blood, lymph and sexual. It fortifies the immune system and promotes the absorption of calcium. In some colour therapies orange light is used as a first-aid treatment for shock and trauma. Try looking into orange if you have just had an argument or an accident.

Yellow is the colour of the mind, a cerebral, left-brain, thinking stimulant.it is linked to strengthening the nervous system, cleaning the liver and the gallbladder. The associations with communication, logic and organisation help dispel fears and nervousness, and promote a sense of order and of being in control. As yellow moves into gold, it is the colour symbolic of higher wisdom and inner radiance. It brings with it hope and a positive, sun-filled, illuminating aspect. Yellow can also be associated with emotions. Its position in the centre of the body (*see page 34*) body relates to the pancreas and our nervous system; in the place where we feel 'butterflies in the tummy'. It is also perhaps where our 'yellow streak' resides.

For the best results, balance orange with blue and yellow with violet.

Before you turn over the page to look at the orange and yellow plant selection, just take a moment to look at this page. Close your eyes and let the impression remain with you. Just quietly decide how this colour makes you feel and what thoughts come into your mind.

orange and yellow

the flowers

Agrimony/*Agrimonia eupatoria*
The herb of sovereign power, 'the flower of perception'. A digestive tonic and astringent used to tone the stomach, liver and gallbladder. It speeds healing of wounds. An infusion makes a good eyewash.
Yellow – Growing wild in open summer woodland and hedges. Fragrance is confined to heavy clay soils

Anise/*Pimpinella anisum*
The orange-and-gold oil colour is a general tonic, promoting clear thought and freeing of the emotions. Use leaves in salads and fruit salads and seeds as an anise spice.
Orange – Sow in open ground after frost risk is past. Harvest dry seeds in autumn.

Buttercup family/*Ranunculaceae*
Winter aconite/*Eranthis hyemalis*
Marsh marigold/*Caltha palustris*
Family members are all good in the wildlife garden as an early and consistent source of pollen and nectar. Symbolically it is for those who undervalue themselves.
Yellow and Orange – In full or partial shade will spread easily in almost any soil. Marsh marigold needs constant moisture.

California poppy/*Eschsholzia californica*
The poppy-like flower of gold. A cousin to the opium poppy, this flower makes a remedy to calm and relax, for internal and external pain. The essence helps to develop a more solid and reliable inner life.
Yellow and Orange – Frost-hardy but needs warm conditions in deep, well-drained soil.

Coriander/*Coriandrum sativum*
Use the leaves and seeds as a vegetable and garnish, and for flavouring. Herbally it is for tiredness, weakness, lack of motivation. Coriander has been used as an aphrodisiac and it is said to encourage optimism and enthusiasm.
Yellow – Sow successionally through spring and summer in light, well-drained soil in full sun.

Cotton lavender/*Santolina chamaecyparissus*
Use as a dwarf hedge or to edge a border or herb garden. Filigree leaves are scented.
Yellow and Orange – Frost hardy, requiring sun and not too rich draining soil.

Cowslip/*Primula veris*
The flower of keys. Rare and protected. Used for making wine and as an ingredient of cheese and cakes. Sacred to Freya the Key Goddess as her love potion. Both root and flowers have been used as a nervous-system tonic. Homeopaths recommend it for negativity.
Yellow – Cowslip will grow almost anywhere, so it is odd that it is endangered, but loss of a natural, chemical-free habitat is the most likely cause. Try it in the front of the border.

Daffodil/*Narcissus pseudonarcissus*
Everyone's favourite, the archetypal English spring flower. Victorian Valentine cards depicted it for 'regards'. So beautiful that a 'nymph fell in love with it'.
Yellow – Fully hardy, in sun or light shade and well-drained soil.

Evening primrose/*Oenothera biennis*
The flower of silent love. Flower stems and leaves make a soothing lotion. Herbally a mild sedative for indigestion, colic, asthma and deep coughs. Homoeopathically, for PMS, the liver, high cholesterol and blood pressure.
Yellow – Fully to frost-hardy, needs full sun and well-drained sandy soil

Fennel/*Foenicullum vulgare*
Thought to have a quality of confidence and assertiveness. Given herbally as an anti-toxin, for indigestion, fluid retention, irregular or painful menses. Best known for cooking, it is also a slimming aid and diuretic. Use the seeds to make a tea.
Yellow – A fully to frost-hardy perennial herb for the border, preferring an open sunny position and fertile, well-drained soil.

Geum/*Geum montanum*
Renowned for its wonderful orange glow.
Orange – A hardy perennial border plant; prefers sun and most well-drained soils.

Goldenrod/*Solidago virgaurea*
Easily influenced by family or social morés? Need to gain approval? Then grow goldenrod to rediscover your identity. A great favourite of Irish herbalists for lax bowels, it has an astringent, bitter taste.
Yellow – A fully hardy perennial, tolerating sun or shade in any draining soil.

Heartsease/*Viola tricolour*
The wild pansy, flower of thoughts. 'For affairs of the heart, a cordial lifts the spirits'. Used in *A Midsummer Night's Dream* for Titania's love potion. It is cooling, cleansing and anti-inflammatory.
Yellow and Purple – A plant of cultivated places, fully hardy, preferring sun and a well-drained soil.

Honeysuckle/*Lonicera caprifolium*
The flower of unity. The Chinese believe that prolonged use prolongs life. Only 12 species are used medicinally, for colds, fevers, headaches and pains. A tea of the leaves can be taken. Homeopathically it is used for irritability and temper.
Orange – Climber on walls, hedges or trees. Fully hardy to frost tender. Grow in fertile or well-drained soil, in sun or semi-shade.

Lady's mantle/*Alchemilla vulgaris*
The flower of alchemy. Has been known as a reproductive tonic and for relief of trauma after abortion or miscarriage. A vaginal douche lotion. Homoeopathically, to be more in touch with our feminine nature.
Yellow – Fully hardy, they grow in all but boggy soils, in sun or partial shade.

Mahonia aquifolium
The flower of acceptance. The root is used to treat liver and gallbladder, to detoxify and relieve fatigue. A cooling and drying effect, it is also used to treat varicose veins.
Yellow – An evergreen shrub, fully to half-hardy, preferring shade or semi-shade, a fertile but not too dry soil.

Mimulus guttatus

'To brighten the dark waterways'. For those fearful of everyday things, of death or old age. Also for people who are very shy.
Yellow and Orange – Fully to half-hardy, prefers sun and wet or moist soil.

Mullein/*Verbascum* 'Cotswold Queen'

The flower of inner light. Derives from the Latin meaning 'soft'. Has cooling properties. Excellent remedy for respiratory system, for coughs and dry throats, asthma, swollen glands. It is smoked for bronchial complaints. The soft downy leaves were used in the Middle Ages to line shoes.
Orange – Fully to frost-hardy, prefers open sunny sites but will tolerate semi-shade, in well-drained soil.

Nasturtium/*Tropaeolum majus*

The flower of patriotism, has a peppery smell. A good blood cleanser, invigorating the digestive system. Use petals in salads, seeds as capers. All parts are edible, rich in iron and Vitamin C. A good tonic, nourishing, detoxifying and immune enhancing.
Orange – One of the easiest and most rewarding to grow. Sow seed in poor soil, in full sun in early summer.

Primrose/*Primula vulgaris*

A universal token of spring, 'the first flower of the year', given at Easter. Used in homoeopathy as a remedy for unexpressed emotion, recently for Seasonal Affective Disorder (SAD).
Yellow – A plant of the hedge banks, grows almost anywhere in moist, draining soil.

St John's Wort/*Hypericum*

The flower of light, to protect against the dark. Bring light into your winter life by taking a few daily drops of the essence. There are many new and old claims. For SAD, for the nerves, for shock and trauma; it may interfere with the production of retro-viruses.
Yellow – Fully to half-hardy perennial, in sun or semi-shade with fertile soil, not too dry.

Snapdragon/*Antirrhinum majus*

Such a sensuous flower to see and touch. Its essence is used for over-powerful, strong-willed people who are aggressive Homoeopathically, it also relieves tension.
Yellow – Fully to half-hardy, needs sun and rich well-drained soil.

With orange we develop self-confidence and self-respect. Yellow is the colour of the mind, a cerebral, left-brain-thinking stimulant.

Pot marigold/*Calendula officinalis*

Flower of the sun, radiant, loving and wise. Used in ointments for healing cuts, stings and burns, as an antiseptic and astringent or to stimulate the immune system. It is anti-viral for flu and herpes and an anti-bacterial for the bowel and all fungal infections. Do not use during pregnancy.
Orange – Annuals and evergreens. Fully hardy to frost tender. Grow in sun and any well-drained soil.

Sunflower/*Helianthus annus*

The flower of the Incas. Universally praised as a symbol of the sun. Once considered better than quinine for malaria. Seeds are highly nutritious.
Yellow – They absorb water and therefore dry out wet soils. Fully hardy, they prefer sun and draining soil.

Wallflower/*Erysitimum cheiri*

The flower of fidelity. Gilli flower, Milk Maids in Greek, means 'hands and flowers'. Steiner said that the seeds contain cardiac glycosides which help establish natural rhythm. A female remedy, but not for home use, but perfume is recommended.
Orange – A perennial, growing on old walls and amongst rocks, in sun and any well-drained soil.

green and white

Green is nature's healing, balancing and restorative colour. It is one of the few constants that personify nature. All other colours come and go but green is reliable, consistent and normalising. It is the colour of new life, and harmony.

Think about the uplifting effect of a green light: imagine a conservatory with a vine covering the roof, the green light, an almost iridescent glow shinning through and filling the room. There is a soothing tranquillity, restful, with a sense that it is here that you can learn to trust the process of life. There is time for everything, physical and emotional space. The Chinese tradition denotes green as the colour of discernment, the ability to make calm, sound judgements. In colour therapies green is used to aid relaxation in every way, a calming force for shock, cooling for headaches and soothing for digestion.

Green is perhaps the most effective healing colour, but it is balanced by red. Lighter greens are balanced by pinks.

In this context we call **white** a colour because it is the light that contains all other colours. When we see an object that appears to be white, it does so because it is reflecting colour wavelengths that are visible to our human eyes.

White is the purifier, the all-cleansing agent that is activating the life force throughout our body, mind and spirit system. White light is said to help us connect with higher consciousness, to elevate ourselves to a state of grace and enlightenment. By growing the white energised flowers and plants and making use of their beneficial light vibrations.

Before you turn over the page to look at the green plant selection, just take a moment to look at this page. Close your eyes and let the impression remain with you. How does this colour make you feel. Can you associate the colour with a taste?

green and white

the flowers

Green is nature's healing, balancing and restorative colour. White is the purifier, the all-cleansing agent that is activating the life force throughout our body, mind and spirit system.

green and white

Angelica/*Angelica archangelica*
The flower of inspiration. 'The root of the Holy Ghost', Angel Grass. Stimulates circulation, warms and invigorates. A superior tonic tea for women.
White and Green – Fully hardy, grows in sun or shade in any well-drained soil.

Basil/*Ocimum basilicum*
From the Latin and Greek, the name means 'royal'. A cleansing and clearing, restorative remedy for digestion and respiratory systems. A versatile culinary herb with a sweet and pungent aroma.
White and Green Easy to grow. Raise from seed annually, in a sunny, fertile position.

Blackberry/*Rubus fruticosus*
The archetypal wild fruit. A sweet leaf tea and fine soft fruit.
White and Blue – A scrambling climber, support young plants. Prefers sun or semi-shade and fertile, well-drained soil.

Box/*Buxus sempervirens*
'To connect you with a spiritual haven', it has many sacred associations. An excellent pollution-resistant plant for pruning into shape as a hedging or topiary sculpture.
Green – Very slow growing, fully to frost-hardy, in sun or semi-shade and any draining soil.

Chamomile/*Chamaemelum nobile; Anthemis nobilis*
Scented Mayweed/*Matricaria chamomilla*
The flower of equilibrium. An infusion reduces inflammation and fevers, is a sedative and calmative. A good bedtime drink. It remedies other ailing garden plants.
White and Blue – Fully to frost-hardy, prefers sun and well-drained soil.

Chickweed/*Stellaria media*
The flower of prediction. The whole plant is highly nutritious containing vitamins A and C and minerals copper and iron. The leaves are perfect in salads, and are cooked like spinach. The arial parts as a herbal are cooling and soothing for the digestion, liver and gall bladder and as a compress or ointment for inflammatory skin complaints.

White and Green – The plant is highly invasive, generally a gardener's bane and can be controlled only in a container. Liking full sun it will flourish in almost any fertile, draining soil.

Crow garlic/*Allium vineale*
The flower of power. Sisters to cultivated garlic, *A. sativum*, the leaves are larger and flowers are more pronounced. They have the ability to purify and drive away infection. Try the leaves in peanut-butter sandwiches. Stimulating and energy giving.
White and Pink – Plants of the woodland floor and hedgerow, they like partial shade and moist soil.

Daisy/*Bellis perennis*
The flower of innocence. The favourite of children and symbol of fidelity, the perennial beauty. Famous as a wound herb, used on the battlefields to staunch bleeding. 'Poor Man's Arnica', used for bruises and shock.
White and Green – Slow-growing perennial, fully hardy in sun or shade and fertile well-drained soil.

Feverfew/*Tanacetum parthenium*
The flower of relief. Ruled by Venus it is said to 'succour our sisters'. Used for headaches and migraine, it helps to clear toxins and heat. A tea used for allergies such as hay fever and asthma.
White and Green – Grows in any soil, self-seeding and spreading easily.

Gardenia/*Gardenia Megasperma*
Purifying the emotions, cleansing of the spirit and auric protection. It is said the oil opens channels of communication. Wonderful perfume.

White and Green – Not easy to grow, they are frost tender, preferring partial shade and humus-rich, neutral to acid, lime-free soil. Try them in containers that can be moved to protect them.

Hawthorn/*Crataegus oxyacantha*; C. *monogyna*
The flower of the heart. Best known as a heart remedy, the flowers, leaves and berries act as a tonic for high blood pressure and to open hardened arteries. A astringent effect for diarrhoea and a digestive relaxant. Early sprouting leaves are great in salads and the flowers and berries are an early and late food for insects and birds.
White and Green – Excellent as a hedge barrier. Fully hardy, preferring sun in any well-drained soil.

Holly/*Ilex aquifolium*
The flower of goodwill, associated with the winter solstice and berries at Christmas. Long known as an early substitute for tea, it has a diaphoretic effect, bringing blood to the skin surface. This causes sweating and is therefore good for fevers and rashes.
White and Green – Fully to half-hardy, preferring draining soil, in sun or shade.

Hops/*Humulus lupulus*
The flower for restful sleep. The sedative action explains why hops are put in pillows. They reduce tension and anxiety. The tannins aid irritated and inflamed conditions of digestion and the bowel. Oestrogen action makes them good for menopause.
White and Yellow – It needs supports, trees or trellis to climb. It's vigorous and so is used to cover walls or sheds. Fully hardy, prefers sun and any well-drained soil.

Ivy/*Hedera helix*

The climbing 'enemy of the vine' it was used to prevent drunkenness – wreaths were worn on the head. The berries are to be avoided, a powerful purgative, destroying red blood cells. Leaves are used for poultices to hasten healing or kill parasites.

White and Green – Trailing perennial and self-clinging climber. Fully to half-hardy, it does well in shade, a northern wall perhaps.

Jasmine/*Jasminum officinale; J. grandiflorum*

The flower of luxury. In Ayurvedic medicine it is used for calming nerves and soothing emotional problems. Perfume is heady.

White and Green – A scrambling climber, frost tender, with some hardy varieties, prefers full sun and fertile draining soil. Plant near the house or by a path.

Lily of the valley/*Convallaria majalis*

One of the most beautiful fragrances, but the plant is also one of the most poisonous.

White and Green – Fully hardy, growing in shade and moist, humus-rich or poor soil.

Meadowsweet/*Filipendula* ulmaria

The flower of late summer meadows. Sweet almond scent of damp ground, a favourite strewing herb. Salicylic acid, a constituent of Aspirin, comes from the plant.

White – Frost-hardy in moisture-retentive soil, in sun or shade.

Nettle/*Urtica dioica*

The flower of spite. 'Now he wants us to encourage nettles'! And it's true, but this is such a useful plant, if you keep it under control. It is a food, a famous soup, a beer, a cheese ingredient, a medicine, rich in vitamins A and C, iron and potassium. Try it as a cleansing spring tonic, taking the new leaves as a tea. It is also good mulch and pesticide wash and is one of the best wildlife attractors.

White and Green – Grows in any draining ground, in sun or shade.

Nicotiana alata; N. sylvestris

The tobacco plant, that releases its scent in the evenings. Its essence is known to benefit people who need strength to face the modern world, to enhance appreciation of the subtle in life.

White and Green – Frost hardy to tender. Needs sun and fertile, draining soil.

Ramsons/*Allium ursinum*

Strong odour and flavour. Can drive away infection.

White and Green – May carpet floor of deciduous woodland. Likes partial shade and moist soil.

Sea Kale/*Crambe maritima*

A spring vegetable delicacy, fresh shoots, roots and seeds. Lifting roots in autumn they will sprout in the dark in winter.

White and Green – Fully hardy in full sun, in any well-drained soil.

Snowdrop/*Galanthus nivalis*

Symbol of life and hope. The name sounds like 'galant'. Sometimes an emblem of death and new life. Such a welcome sight, the 'Candlemass Bell' is often the first bloom to appear after the coldest weather.

White and Pink – Plant bulbs in the autumn. Fully to frost-hardy, they prefer the cool of partial shade in humus rich and moist soil.

Yarrow/*Achillea millefolium*

The flower of invulnerability. A yarrow tea is excellent for the digestion, enhancing appetite and absorption. Stimulates circulation and perspiration, reducing fevers and detoxifying. Folklore history has it staunching bleeding and as anti-inflammatory and antiseptic.

White – Fully hardy, tolerates most soils, prefers sun and well-drained soil.

Valerian/*Valeriana officinalis*

Culpepper calls it 'the most perfect herbal sedative'. The root is used as an homoeopathic remedy for anxiety.

White and Pink – A perennial herb to plant in spring in any well-drained soil. Fully hardy, it prefers sun.

blue, indigo and violet

In relation to the effects of colour in the garden, **blue** must be subdivided into light or sky blue and a deeper blue, indigo.

Blue encourages us to centre ourselves, to be still, calm and clear, allowing our intuition to be heard. Blue is the colour of the sea, the symbolic realm of the unconscious. **Light blue** contains anti-bacterial properties and is also beneficial for easing headaches, back pain and menstrual pain. Part of the rational for these ideas comes from association: the sky is clear when it's blue, therefore it is believed that blue is a good colour to treat eye problems. The sea actually appears blue because it reflects the sky and therefore it is said that blue encourages reflection and so helps to lead to inner peace.

Deep blue or **indigo** is more protective and authoritative, symbolising knowledge with understanding. Like the lighter blue, it cools, but is more intense and therefore heals deeper pain. Indigo is used for treating burns, bruises and neuralgia. In some ancient beliefs, indigo is said to open the third eye, allowing intuition, higher reasoning and ecstatic vision to enter. Looking at deep blue can be a good sedative, producing a kind of anaesthesia. It is therefore beneficial in relieving painful stress.

Violet is associated with the spirit, and the divinity and the power of kings. It is the colour of powerful self knowledge. Vibrating at a high frequency, it is protective of the mind. Violet is said to dissolve fears. Containing both red from the base and higher blue, it is the transforming colour, harmonising our base functions with the higher mind and spirit. Identified as a psychological primary colour by traditional colour scientists, it has been used for healing mental and nervous disorders. Physically, it is effective for over-activity, repairing exhaustion by normalising glandular and hormonal functions. It is a blood purifier, assisting the building of white blood cells for immunity. By regulating the balance of potassium and sodium, it helps to maintain our water balance and heart rhythms.

While a violet hue is quite easy to create in the garden, the blues can be a little more difficult to create for the gardener.

Before you turn over the page to look at the blue plant selection, just take a moment to look at this beautiful colour. Close your eyes and let the impression remain with you. Are you reminded of an emotion?

blue, indigo and violet

the flowers

Autumn gentian/*Gentiana amarella*
The flower of bitterness. For those who are easily discouraged. Contains one of the most bitter substances in the plant world. Herbally it is used for digestion and as a strengthening detoxifier.
Violet and Red – A large perennial herb for the rock garden or peat bed. Fully hardy, they prefer sun or semi-shade, in humus rich and draining neutral to acid soil.

Bluebell *Hyacinthoides endymion; H. non-scripta*
An endangered species as their habitat disappears. Can you look at a bluebell wood without your spirits lifting?
Blue and Violet – Fully hardy spring-flowering bulbs for borders and naturalising in grass under trees. Needs partial shade and moisture.

Blue poppy/*Meconopsis grandis*
The purest blue possible in the garden.
Blue – Fully hardy, needs shade and a cool position, in humus-rich, moist and neutral to acid soil.

Borage/*Borago officinalis*
The blue 'star flower'. A wonderful herb with many uses. Always brings courage and dispels melancholy. Herbally primes the body for dangerous and stressful times. Put flowers in your Pimms and salads.
Blue – Fully hardy perennial and annual, preferring sun and fertile, draining soil.

Buddleia/*Buddleja davidii*
The butterfly bush. Famous for its attraction to butterflies and insects.
Violet and Blue – Almost anyone can grow it. Prune hard in spring for the best late summer flowers. Fully hardy, prefers sun and well-drained soil.

Campanula lactiflora
An intense blue-violet for the border.
Blue and Violet – Annuals and perennials, some evergreen. half-hardy in sun or shade, (shading will preserve the flowers) needing rich moist soil.

Catmint/*Nepeta cataria*
The flower of cats. Popular in England before tea was imported. Similar herbal action to Camomile.
Violet and Blue – A summer-flowering perennial, for edging and tumbling over paving. Fully hardy, preferring sun and moist, well-draining soil.

Clematis montana alba; C. viticella; C. x 'Mrs Cholmondeley'
Vigorous climbing plants with a wide variety of sizes and shades.
Blue and Violet – Clematis needs pruning to control it. Pruning – if it flowers before mid-summer, prune it after flowering to the bud nearest the main growth. If it flowers after mid-summer, prune it near to the ground in mid-winter. Fully to half-hardy. Grow in shade or full sun. Prefers shaded roots and rich, well-drained soil.

Cornflower/*Centaurea cyanus*
Herbally used as an eyebath for soothing and ulcers. Bees and birds are attracted.
Blue and Violet – Fast growing and upright, excellent for cutting, hardy annual liking sun and well-drained soil.

Digitalis purpurea
(*D. lanata* contains digoxin)
The leaves, warmed in hot water and rolled as a poultice will relieve earache and headache. The grey flower variety contains the famous heart medicine.
Violet – Fully hardy, preferring partial shade and woodland-like conditions.

Forget-me-not family *Borago*; *Myosotis*; *Anchusa*
Includes wood and field varieties, Borage and Bugloss.
Blue – As with Borage but liking moisture and more humus.

Geranium 'Johnson's Blue'
Cranesbill. The essence encourages harmony and tranquillity. Herbally cooling and soothing for bruises, for anxiety and overexcitement. A good insect-repellent.
Blue – Low-growing mats of flowers and foliage. Must have full sun, in any soil.

Honesty/*Lunaria rediviva*
Really for texture and visual pleasure. Beautiful dried seeds in winter.
Blue and Violet – Fully hardy, in sun or shade, in fertile, well-drained soil.

Hyssop/*Hyssopus officinalis*
The flower of forgiveness. A versatile medicine for purification and invigoration. Herbally for skin bruising and dermatitis, for pain relief and grief.
Blue and Violet – A small shrub member of the mint family. Grows almost anywhere.

Juniper/*Juniperus communis*
Good for toxic conditions, cystitis and poor appetite. Flavouring in gin, and a fine little used culinary herb. Surprisingly good for hangovers. Avoid during pregnancy.
Violet and Blue – Coniferous shrubby tree, with peeling bark. Fully hardy in an open site, in fertile dry soil.

Larkspur/*Consolida ajacis* 'Bluetit'
The essential cottage-garden flower. A herbal eye wash: 'trouble free eyes for the year to come'. Essence relieves a sense of over-burdening.
Blue and Violet – Stake as they grow tall, in rich, well fed draining soil, in sun with shelter.

Lavender/*Lavandula officinalis*
One of the most famous blue calmatives, it calms the heart and lowers blood pressure. From the Latin, 'lavare' or to wash.
Blue and Violet – Trim after flowering. Edging to the herb garden or lining paths. Fully to half-hardy, likes full sun and fertile, well-drained soil.

Mahonia x media
Deep blue berries and yellow scented flowers in winter.
Blue and Yellow – Fully to half-hardy, preferring shade and a fertile, moist but well-drained soil.

Myrtle/*Myrtus communis*
A nosegay for the sick room, and the berries produce a wax on them that is used as scented candle wax.

Blue is the colour of the sea, the symbolic realm of the unconsciousness. Indigo is more protective and authoritative, symbolising knowledge with understanding. Violet is the colour of powerful self knowledge.

Blue and Green – Must have a sunny, sheltered position to flower and fruit. Often frost tender, containers suit it well with any draining soil.

Onions and garlic/*Allium*

The flowers of power. The 'Heal All'. They are antibiotic, used as expectorants, for thrombosis, worms, diabetes, to relieve nervousness and insecurity. A strong purifier and fine everyday vegetable.
Blue and White – Look for the modified bulbs to grow in colder climes. Leave undisturbed to form clumps. Fully to frost-hardy, in open, sunny and well-drained soil.

Pasque flower/*Pulsatilla vulgaris*

The flower of forsakeness. Dried flowers, in an infusion, are used as a nerve tonic, and for relaxation and a good night's sleep.
Violet and Blue – Fully hardy, needs full sun and humus-rich draining soil.

Periwinkle/*Vinca major; V. minor*

The flower of closeness. 'Joy of the Ground'. For love philtres to ensure a happy marriage, flowers are strewn in the path of the bride. A great 'binder', it can be chewed. Reduces excessive menstrual bleeding, tension and blood sugar.
Violet – Fully to frost-hardy. Ground cover in shade, flowers in sun. In any watered soil.

Prunella vulgaris

Self-Heal, the flower of confidence. Used as a gargle for sore throats and mouth ulcers. Also a tea for headaches and over sensitivity to light. Member of the mint family much loved by bees.
Violet – Suitable for rock gardens. Fully hardy in sun or shade and moist, well-drained soil.

Rosemary/*Rosmarinus officinalis*

The flower of loyalty. The herb of vitality. It is antiseptic and astringent. Used for skin problems, ageing, a nerve tonic and for increasing warmth and confidence. Do not use during pregnancy or with high blood pressure. Many culinary uses and for fruit cups and mulled wine.
Violet and Green – An herbaceous perennial needing a warm protected spot in well-drained soil.

Sage/*Salvia officinalis*

The flower of immortality, it was seen to cure so many ills. Cleansing, purifying for surface infections. Highly antiseptic, anti-bacterial and anti-fungal. Sage tea is remedy for colds and coughs. It was used to treat TB.
Violet and Blue – Prefers sun and fertile, well-drained soil.

Snake's Head Fritillary/*Fritillaria meleagris*

A beautiful endangered species of the damp water meadows, with delicate spring flowers. Provides nectar for early butterflies.
Blue and Violet – Perennial bulbs planted in autumn. Needs a damp and shady place.

Violet/*Viola odorata*

The flower of shyness. For those who are nervous or timid. Symbol of peace, faith and piety. To open the heart so that other people don't appear so threatening. The essence has a soporific effect, a cooling action where there is heat or inflammation. Said to restore libido especially during menopause.
Violet and Blue – In sun or partial shade and fertile, draining soil.

Wisteria/*Sinensis floribunda*

As an Australian bush essence, it is known for those who deny their sexuality and femininity and who fear intimacy.
Violet – For walls and pergolas, against buildings and trees. Fully to frost-hardy needing full, south-facing sun and fertile draining soil.

sound – harmony and nature

Natural sounds are universally calming

In the 1920's, the spiritual philosophers Gurdjieff and Ouspensky held a number of special music-and-sound concerts for the fashionable elite of Paris. They played sequences of notes to the audience believing that certain specific combinations of notes and sounds could elicit a precise and common emotional response. We are not told in their reports of the concerts whether they were indeed successful. Certainly, however, they believed that they were making their audiences react similarly to the same stimulus, crying or laughing together simply by playing them particularly evocative sounds. It is similar to the effect of listening to a pieces of music that make us feel elated or sad, and there are many pieces of popular music that are commonly recognised as being emotionally evocative. It is believed that in the garden, the sound of running or babbling water has a calming effect. Listening to the wind rustle leaves and grasses or to the clacking of bamboo are also known to aid peace and help with focusing the mind.

In the Chinese art of Feng Shui it is thought that if the universal energy is stagnating, it can be broken up and redistributed using sound. Chimes of metal and bamboo are often employed to do this. In an urban setting, with all of the accompanying ambient synthetic and continuous noise pollution, it is reasonable to assume that natural sounds will counteract the negative effects. Consequently, this will encourage wildlife, birdsong or the buzzing of insects, to promote a restful atmosphere.

sound *as therapy*

Our hearing is amazingly acute and just as we understand the positive and negative effects of the different frequency vibrations of colours, with sound it is perhaps easier to understand how we can feed ourselves positive sound vibrations.

Many of the presently available colour therapies combine the frequencies of sound as it is thought that there is a distinct correlation between them. The effect of red, for example, is thought to be enhanced by the notes C and B, green by F and F#, blue by A and E and orange by D and G. These sounds are said to penetrate deeply into the body tissues and promote well being. This is similar to the concept of singing or speaking to an unborn child in the womb.

sounds *in the garden*

The word 'listen' is an anagram of silent.

Using water in the garden is one of the best ways to promote calm, and encouraging natural sound improves our well being.

The Steiner-inspired flow form is perhaps the best example of therapeutic and aesthetic water use. It makes the right sounds, and its shape, which controls the flow circulation, is said to be perfect for invigorating and energising the water's nutritional properties. Supplied with a submersible pump, they all can be driven from a catchment pond which can be as small as an old sink or a barrel. Another water feature to try is the Japanese bamboo pipe, the water trickling into a pot not only produces an enchanting sound but is also an unusual sculpture.

Grasses, leaves and seed pods are very effective natural sound producers. From the bamboos in a larger garden, *Phyllostachys viridiglaucescens* and *Phyllostachys nigra*, and the smaller variety, *Sinarundinaria nitida*, to the smaller grasses, *Miscanthus*, which has many varieties including the pink variety, *M. sinensis* 'Kleine Fontäne'. The pampas grass species are popular: *Cortaderia selloana* from New Zealand is one of the most common. Seed pods like the 'Bladder Senna', *Colutea arborescens*, or the seed heads of poppies, will produce a rattle and rustle in the wind.

The introduction of sound adds so much to a garden and often goes hand in hand with movement. Beyond the plants that respond to the wind, consider trees like aspen and poplars that flutter, such as whispering willows and pines.

Hearing a sound
without seeing its
source can produce a
beguiling magic.

aroma – the perfume garden

Perfume in the garden evokes memories and romantic associations. The aroma of scented plants on a summers evening is guaranteed to instill a sense of well-being

As our understanding of the effects of aroma on our health grows, we can add yet another dimension to garden sanctuary. The origins of aromatherapy can be traced back more than 5,000 years. As a bathing treat or for massage, to purify the atmosphere, attract a lover or please the gods. Specific therapy with essential oils, however, is a relatively new art. In practice many plant essences can be prescribed in the same way as herbs, for example a calmative such as coriander oil for indigestion or marjoram oil as an anti-spasmodic for asthma. The difference is in the highly volatile and ethereal nature of the oil which appears to have a profound effect on our mental and emotional state. Certainly an important factor in its efficacy as a

psychological therapy is our actual perception of fragrance and our response to it. From chamomile to treat anger, hyssop for grief, rose for jealousy, it is interesting that these essences are now being widely used not only to stimulate and relax but also to treat many types of internal disease. Research has found, for example, that bergamot, chamomile and lavender possess a property which stimulates the production of white blood cells. Engaging with our immune response, oils are now being used quite conventionally to treat infections or simply to maintain a high level of resistance. Chamomile, for example, contains the chemical azulene, known as an effective anti-inflammatory agent. As the name suggests this chemical is coloured deep blue and, not surprisingly, this is the colour used by colour-therapists to reduce inflammation. It is now thought that rather than simply being a chemical mix, these agents possess a more subtle vibrational frequency, each one having a resonance which corresponds to certain aromas, colours and even sounds.

Cinnamon is a good example as it possesses the colour orange of the sun and fire and, interestingly, it is used by the aromatherapist to warm and stimulate the heart and circulation, causing a rise in body temperature.

Relative sensuality

To the flowers, fragrance may simply be a deterrent to being eaten or an attraction to pollinating insects. For us, so dominated by our visual sense, it would seem a good idea to restore some sensual balance, close our eyes and breathe in.

Originally
designed for the
visually impaired by
Claire Whitehouse,
essential oils
bubbling through
the water release
a stimulating
aroma.

the perfume garden

the flowers

Artemesia vulgaris

The flower of the moon goddess. Used for menstrual problems and in menopause. The leaves and flowers in a bath is a good treatment. It is Moxa, or the warming herb of Chinese traditional medicine.

Situation – Half-hardy, prefers sun and well-drained soil.

Brompton stock/Matthiola incana

White perennial stock, a form of wild stock, easily grown and the most powerfully scented.

Situation – Fully hardy to frost tender, prefers sun or semi-shade, in fertile, lime-rich well-drained soil.

Clematis/Clematis montana; C. vitalba

C. vitalba is the Bach flower remedy for dreamers, helping them to live in the present.

Situation – Fully to half-hardy, happy in shade or full sun, in rich, draining, root-shaded soil.

Common lilac/Syringa vulgaris 'Sensation'

A particular Victorian favourite. One of the most evocative English garden perfumes.

Situation – Fully hardy, prefers sun and deep fertile, alkaline well-drained soil.

Dames violet/Hesperis matronalis

Sweet rocket. Popular cottage garden perfume best in the evening.

Situation – Fully hardy, prefers sun and well-drained soil.

Daphne odora; D. burkwoodii

An evergreen shrub with small but spicily scented flower clusters, flowering in winter when little else can.

Situation – Fully to frost-hardy, preferring full sun and deep fertile, draining but not over-dry soil.

Honesty/Lunaria

See Blue and Violet Colour selection

Hyacinth/Hyacinthus orientalis

In Greek mythology the flower arose from the blood of Apollo's lover. These give winter colour and a balsam perfume in the house.

Situation – For spring bedding or indoor pot cultivation. Plant in autumn. Frost hardy, prefers sun and well-drained soil.

Incense rose/Rosa primula

An early spring rose with a delicate fragrance. In Persia it was believed that the first rose was stirred into life by the rays of the rising sun.

Situation – Fully hardy, prefers sun in open and fertile, moist but draining soil.

Japanese apricot/Prunus mume 'Beni-chidori'

A most beautiful early spring, cherry-like flower.

Situation – Fully hardy in sun or shade and in any but waterlogged soil.

Lemon balm/Melissa officinalis

The flower of bees. Ruling the heart it calms and slows. A good bedtime tea to soothe away troublesome cares. Strong lemon perfume.

Situation – Frost hardy, prefers sun and fertile, draining soil. Plant is easily self-seeding. Plant near the house or by a path.

Lemon verbena/Aloysia triphylla

The leaves are used in fruit salads and punch. Crushed or bruised, they are strongly lemon scented. It is an antiseptic and an insect repellent.

Situation – Half-hardy, needs a warm south aspect, full sun and well-drained soil.

Madonna lily/Lilium candidum

The Flower of Resurrection. Dedicated to the image of the Virgin Mary.

Situation – A summer-flowering bulb. Frost hardy, planted in autumn or spring. Prefers sun and any well-drained soil.

Perfume in the garden is so important. It evokes memories and romantic associations. Is there anything more guaranteed to instill a sense of well-being than a warm evening filled with the scent of Jasmine or stocks.

aroma and perfume

Magnolia/*Magnolia wiesneri; sinensis*

Some of the largest and most fragrant flowers for a temperate climate.
Situation – Fully to frost-hardy, with a risk of flower damage from late frosts. Prefers sun or semi-shade and wind shelter, in fertile, draining soil.

Mexican orange blossom/*Choisya ternata*

With aromatic glossy yellow leaves and fragrant star shaped white flowers.
Situation – Frost hardy, prefers sun and fertile well-drained soil.

Mock orange/*Philadelphus coronarius; P. delavayi*

A long-lasting and sweet-scented graceful bush. A haunting, uplifting orange-like aroma.
Situation – Fully hardy, prefers sun, and fertile well- drained soil.

Passion flower/*Passiflora incarnata*

The flower to pacify. A relaxing remedy for stress. Just to look at the flower is remedy enough.
Situation – half-hardy, a climbing vine, good for containers. Prefers sun or partial shade in fertile, well-watered but draining soil.

Rose geranium/*Pelargonium graveolens*

Commonly grown for its essential oil, as perfume and an aromatherapy. Ideal for stress-related disorders, to relieve tension, anxiety and to lift the spirits.
Situation – Frost tender, prefers a sunny site, but dislikes very hot or humid conditions. Well-drained neutral to alkaline soil.

Solomon's seal/*Polygonatum odoratum*

The 'seal of the blessed Virgin'. A cool woodland spirit, with a beautiful fragrance.
Situation – Fully hardy to frost tender perennial. Needs cool shady, fertile soil that does not dry out.

Spanish broom/*Spartium junceum*

Used in ancient Greek temples, fragrant yellow pea-like flower.
Situation – Fully hardy, needs sun and not too rich, well-drained soil.

Wild marjoram/*Origanum vulgare*

Oregano, the culinary herb of all Mediterranean cuisine, which forms a fragrant mat of ground cover. A warming analgesic infusion.
Situation – Fully hardy, prefers sun and well-drained, alkaline soil.

Winter honeysuckle/*Lonicera fragrantissima*

A winter joy, delicate white fragrant flowers on bare stems.
Situation – Hardy, will grow in shade in any well-drained soil.

Witch hazel/*Hamamelis virginiana mollis; H. x intermedia*

The Flower of Divination. Bright yellow or orange sharply scented flowers from December to February. A general household remedy for burns, skin swelling and inflammation. Stops bleeding.
Situation – Fully hardy, prefers sun or semi-shade, in fertile, peaty, acid, well-drained soil.

aroma – scents and sensibility

The garden generates a mass of wonderful and informative scents. Beyond fragrances of plants situated by the house, or in the places where you are free to pass and can touch regularly, there is the aroma of freshly turned soil, the fresh smell of the garden after rain, or the compost smells which will inform the initiated as to what is happening inside the heap. Most plant scents are almost intentionally agreeable to us. Aromatic compounds in the leaves deter the unwanted grazers while encouraging the needed pollinators. Just smell the tomato plants, the basil or coriander, then try to resist eating them!

Many of the more fragrantly perfumed leaves need brushing to release the scents and beyond simple pleasure, the medicinal aromatic effect will then also be released. The herbal evergreens and pines, the balms such as lemon balm (*Melissa*) will fill the air while on the ground, mint and thyme or a small roman chamomile will grow in the cracks of paths to be stepped on and release their aroma. At night, nicotiana or scented stocks, honeysuckle or viburnum, growing by an open window on summer evenings, will fill the house with glorious perfume.

Lemon balm/*Melissa officinalis*

Famous for its refreshing perfume and flavour, Lemon Balm makes a delicious tea or a cooling addition to fruit salads or drinks. Chopped leaves can be added to salads, sweet jellies, jams and summer puddings, the flavour is sweet and sharp, like lemons and has a positive effect on the limbic system of the brain, which controls mood and temperament. Traditionally, a remedy for stress, anxiety and depression, digestive problems and inflammation. Mild enough to calm children at night, it can also relieve stomach upsets and reduce fevers. It has been used against infections, for allergies such as hay fever and for all kinds of pain, especially menstrual and also as a relaxant before childbirth. It is an antiseptic for cuts and sores and also has anti-viral properties against colds and flu. It is said to calm and uplift the emotions and soothe panic and shock.

Harvest the leaves throughout the summer, as a food ingredient or for teas to drink, or use for refreshing and cleansing lotions. The crushed leaves will make instant compresses, or infused in oil, can be used for massage, as a bath condiment or a perfume. Perhaps one of this plant's best uses is as a bush by a door into the house, where you will regularly brush past and release its fragrance.

Easy to grow in a well-watered sunny position. The warmer the sun, the stronger the perfume. You can propagate it by sowing the seed in April or planting out the seedling after the frost. Prune it back in late autumn to keep it bushy.

Plants used in aromatherapy

- **Basil** *Ocimum basilicum*
Uplifting and stimulating (Avoid in pregnancy and on sensitive skins)
- **Bergamot** *Citrus bergamia*
Refreshing, anti-depressant, antiseptic (Not when skin is exposed to strong sunlight)
- **Camomile** *Chamaemelum nobile*
Refreshing, for pain and fevers, anti-depressant
- **Cedarwood** *Cedrus atlantica*
A sedative
- **Clary Sage** *Salvia sclarea*
Warming and calming, an anti-depressant. (Avoid in pregnancy)
- **Cypress** *Cupressus sempervirens*
Refreshing and a deodorant
- **Eucalyptus** *Eucalyptus globulus*
Warming and antiseptic, expectorant, for fevers
- **Geranium** *Pelargonium odoratissimum*
Refreshing, relaxing and uplifting
- **Juniper** *Juniperus communis*
Refreshing, detoxifying, stimulating (Avoid in pregnancy)
- **Lavender** *Lavandula angustifolia*
Refreshing, relaxing, antiseptic, for pain
- **Melisssa** *Melissa officinalis*
Uplifting and also for fevers (Not on sensitive skins)
- **Peppermint** *Mentha x piperita*
Cooling and stimulating (Avoid in pregnancy and on sensitive skins)
- **Pine** *Pinus sylvestris*
Refreshing and antiseptic
- **Rose** *Rosa x centifolia; R. x damascena*
Relaxing, calming, anti depressant, aphrodisiac (Avoid in pregnancy)
- **Rosemary** *Rosmarinus officinalis*
Invigorating, antiseptic, for pains (Avoid in pregnancy or with high blood pressure)
- **Tarragon** *Artemesia dracunculus*
Warming, invigorating and relaxing
- **Thyme** *Thymus vulgaris*
Antiseptic and anti-bacterial (Not on sensitive skins or with high blood pressure)

touch in the garden

try the blindfold-touch game

touch *is underrated*

It's not just our hands either that are free to engage in this unique relationship, walking barefoot on dew-laden grass or newly raked fine tilth is an experience not to be missed.

Of all our senses, touch is perhaps the most underrated. Through the evolution of man it is the discovery of objects that we touch and form with our hands that drives progress. Take some clay and mould it into a ball, a pot, a figure, a cup.

At first we might feel that the shape has been given to us by nature, but of course, it's not true. This is human made and what the pot does is to reflect the shape of our hand. Similarly the splitting of wood or stone probes and explores beneath the surface and thereby becomes an instrument of our discovery. Our hands are the most fundamental of tools that we use to prise open and discover the nature of the world around us.

As children we played the 'blindfold-touch' game in the garden. After spinning around blindfolded, an object was placed before your expectant hand to touch; bark, furry, hairy leaves, a slug, an apple, a petal, a handful of something! The garden has many tactile sensations to offer.

This sense of touch in the garden can be thought of as something akin to that of a lover. Wear gloves if you like, and sometimes you may need them for protection, but actually placing your hands deep into the earth is really to consummate your relationship with the natural world.

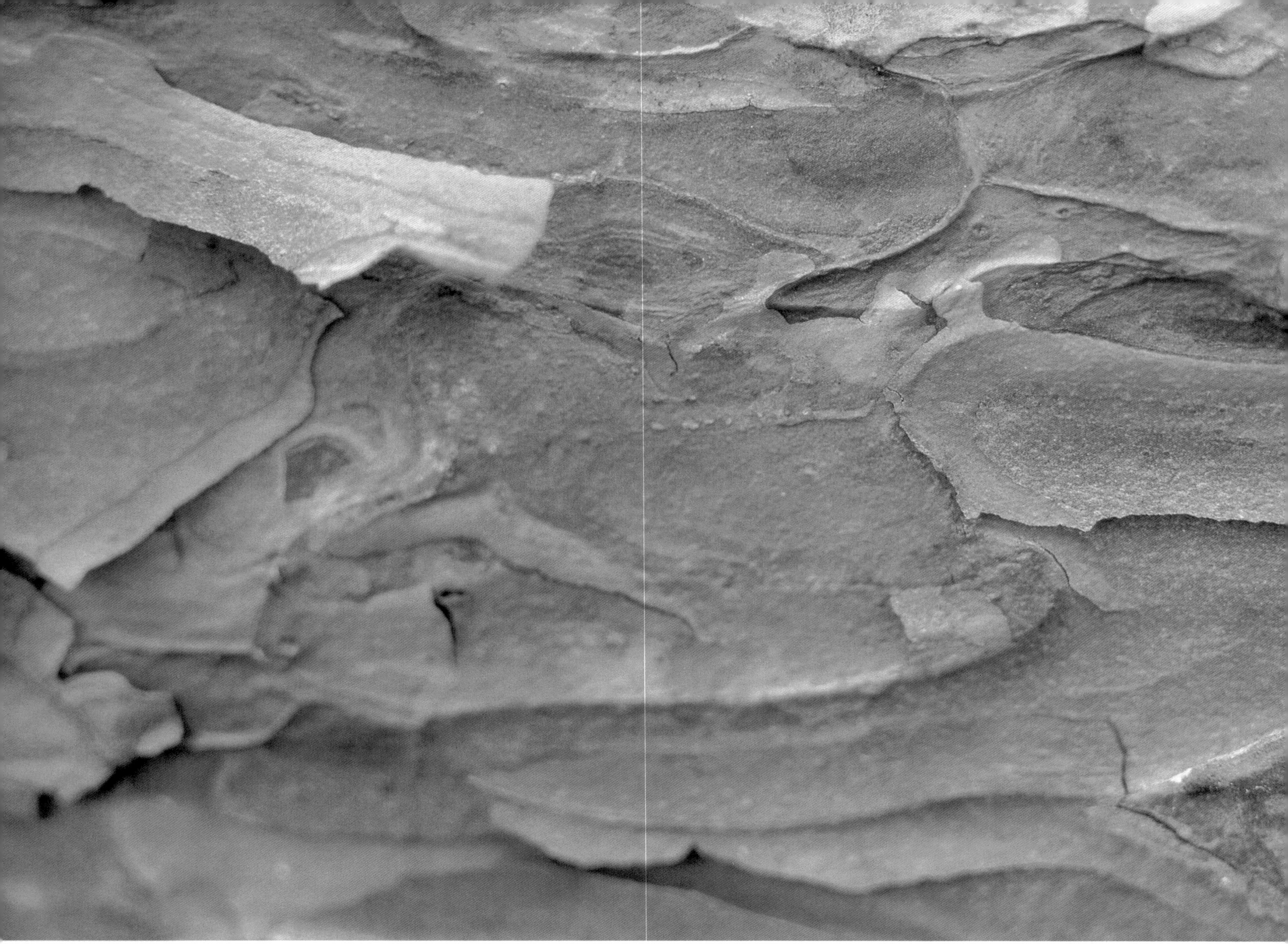

touch – the brain and the hand unite

Exploring the natural world

A popular cliché in philosophy claims that science is only pure analysis, while reductionism and art is only pure synthesis. One can only take the rainbow to pieces, the other can only put it together. But it is not so simple. All of our imagination begins by exploring nature with our hands. Michelangelo echoes this sentiment in his sonnet on the act of creation.

When that which is divine in us doth try

to shape a face, both hand and brain unite

to give, from a mere model frail and slight,

Life to the stone by art's free energy.

The brain and hand unite. The material becomes real through our hands and it is this that stimulates the brain to shape it. Close your eyes when you touch and your imagination is given free reign.

Use a trowel, a spade or fork if you wish, but there is something very special, some deep connections to be found, by parting the earth with your fingers and placing the seed within.

Touch it and see

In order to further enhance our connection with nature, we can easily include the element of touch into our garden sanctuary. Think first about different kinds of base material: earth, clay, sand, stone or gravel, which can be used for a number of purposes in the garden. Cold stone and rock is made warm and living by a covering of moss. Almost any plant has a tactile quality and, indeed, for many gardeners it is second nature to ruffle the leaves and test for dryness or strength and vigour. Particular plants like mullein, *Stachys* or *Salvia argentea* positively invite you to stroke their downy and furrowed leaves.

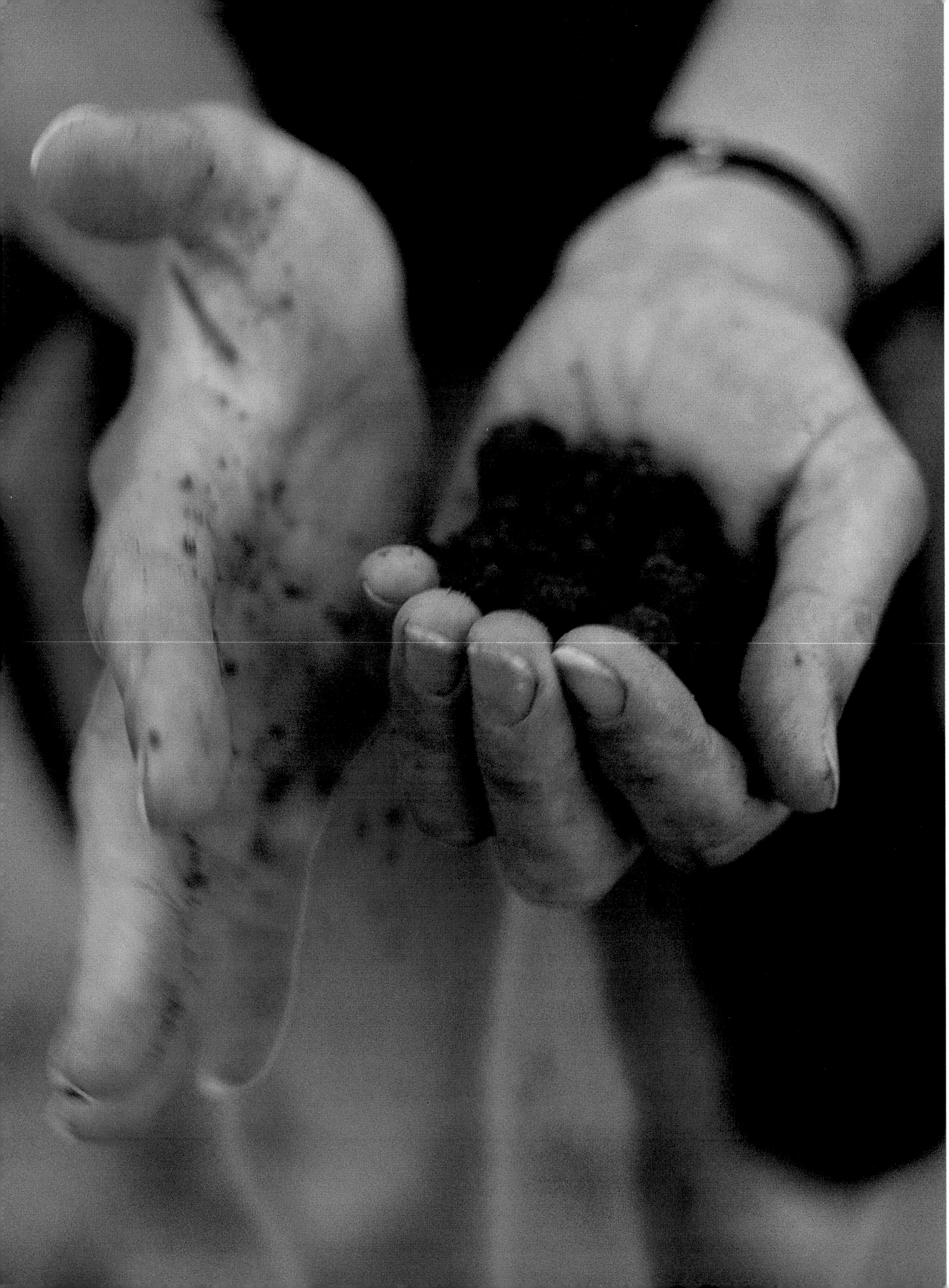

taste treats

food for free

Your garden, no matter how small, is potentially the most fantastic source of flavours and taste treats. So much is written about the vegetable plot; interestingly much expert opinion divides plants and flowers into separate categories, as though the plants are completely different from those in the flower garden. But it all rather depends on your definition of food. A seminal 1970s book called *Food For Free* by Richard Mabey detailed so many food plants that have been long forgotten as wonderful culinary delicacies as well as beautiful flowers. The old idea of the potager cottage garden, where herbs and vegetables are grown amongst, the flowers and architectural forms, would seem to be an ideal way to experience taste and beauty from the garden. There is no attempt here to persuade you to be self-sufficient or to replace what you buy from the supermarket. The plants here are additions, luxury tastes with extra magic because they are special, in small quantity and grown by you. When you come to sit down at your special table, there is no more sacred act than eating these fresh 'fruits' from the larder outside.

Aspiring expert or novice, don't be afraid to experiment and learn; there is plenty of time.

Culinary herbs

The sun brings out the oil and therefore the flavour of culinary herbs. Try making herb vinegars by crushing the herb in a small amount of boiling vinegar. Add an equal amount of cold vinegar and keep for two weeks, regularly shaking. Strain before using.

Bay/*Laurus nobilis*
Add the leaves to cooking pasta, rice, soups, stews and fish dishes.
Frost hardy. Plant seedlings in full sun and fertile, well-drained soil.

Chives/*Allium schoenoprasum*
The Infant Onion. Great chopped with cheese, potato, cucumber and in salads and omelettes.
Sow seed in spring in fertile, well-drained soil. Perfect for container growing or for flowering in the border.

Horseradish/*Amoracia rusticana*
Peel and grate the root. Mix with yoghurt and sugar. A hot and fruity condiment.
Frost hardy. Likes rich and deeply cultivated soil for the root growth. In spring, drop a cut piece of root 30cm (12in) down. Water well. Grow in a container as it can be invasive.

Lovage/*Levisticum officinale*
Its flavour is unusual, a little like celery. Try the young leaf shoots and stems as a cooked vegetable or as an addition to salads, soups and stews.
A tall perennial needing a lot of space. Frost hardy, it likes sun and fertile well-drained soil.

Purslane/*Portulaca oleracea*
Cook the young growth, eat with butter as an hors d'oeuvre like asparagus.
Frost tender. Likes full dun and almost any well-drained soil.

Sweet cicely/*Myrrhis odorata*
Use instead of sugar in all types of cooking and salads. A frost-hardy tall perennial. Sow in spring in open ground. Likes partial shade and moist fertile soil.

Tarragon/*Artemesia dracunculus*
Use for white sauces and vinegar.
Frost tender. Plant seedlings in full sun and well-drained fertile soil. Propagate with cuttings, cut down and mulch in late autumn.

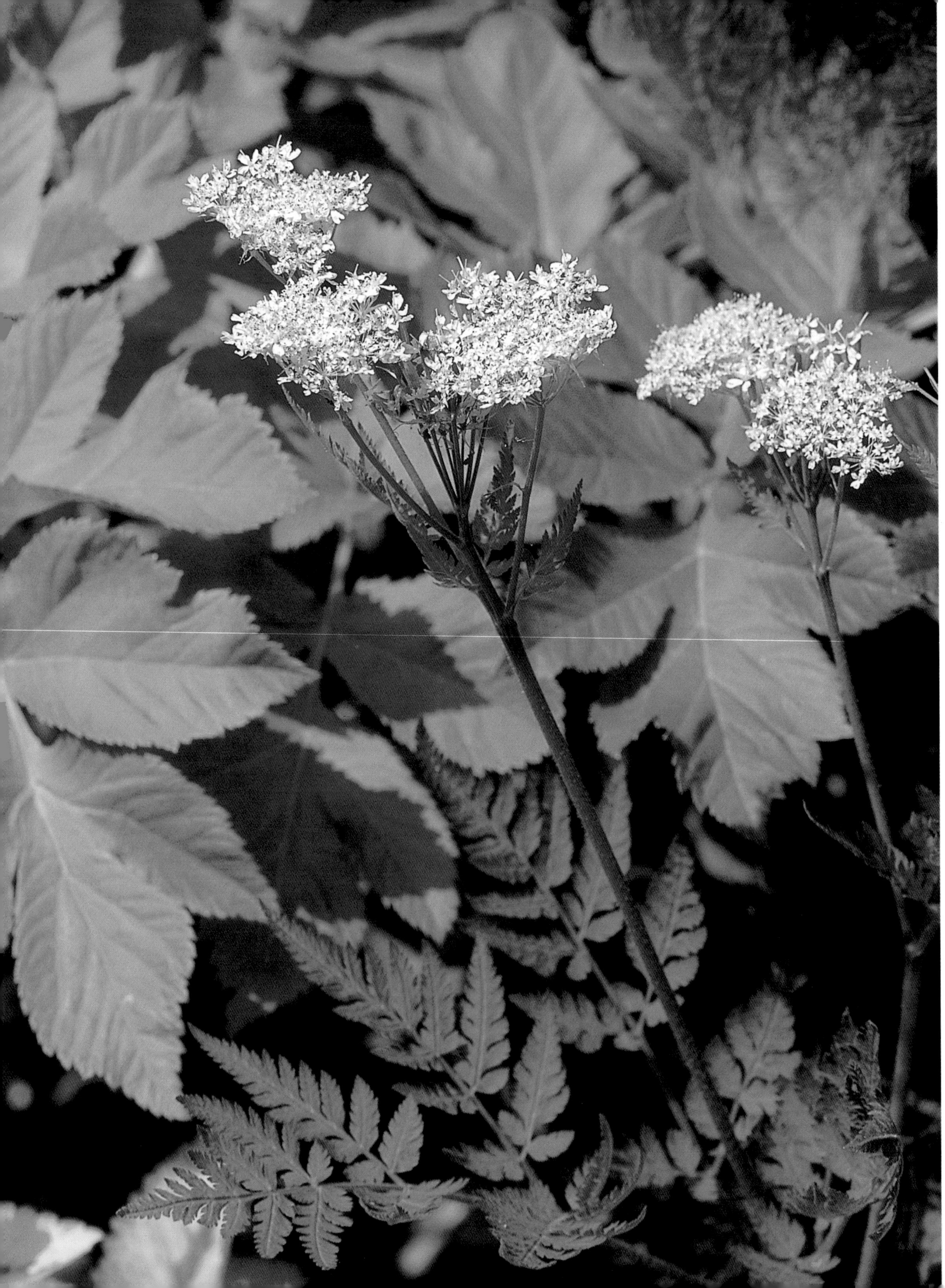

vegetables and fruit

Vegetables

Broad and field beans/
Vicia fabalemon

A soup or salad, cooked and served with and butter. Great as background, use tall 'Aquadulce Claudia' as architecture in the border.

'Red Epicure' has attractive flowers and red beans.

Sow 'Aqua' in autumn and others as soon in spring as the soil is workable, in any fertile, draining soil.

Cabbage/*Brassica*

Red cabbage in the border is beautiful. Good as a staple salad or a cooked vegetable.

Sow under glass from spring to early summer, planting out and protecting seedlings in an open sunny position in fertile, well-manured, draining soil.

Cardoon/*Cynara cardunculus*

Use the young stem inners and cook until tender. Serve as a vegetable with cream and fresh tarragon.

Sow seeds in late spring, 30cm (12in) deep in well-manured draining soil. In late autumn, tie leaves, earth up stems and cover with black polythene. Dig up a month later.

Endive/*Cichorium endivia*

Endive and olive salad is traditional. Like a cross between a cabbage and a lettuce, it is an all-year-round bitter salad vegetable with green and red leaf varieties. Late in the season, earth up around the tied stems to keep them tender.

Sow seeds from early spring to mid-summer in fertile, well-drained soil.

Globe artichoke/*Cynara scolymus*

A delicious hors d'oeuvres. Serve after cooking for 40 minutes in lemon water, with a vinaigrette dressing.

Plant seedlings or suckers in spring. Pluck first-year flower heads for larger heads in the second year. Frost hardy, they like sun and plenty of well-rotted manure.

Lettuces
Lollo Rosso/*Lactuca sativa*
Lamb's Lettuce/*Valerianella locusta*

Summer, autumn and winter salads. They are decorative and versatile.

Frost tender (Lamb's is frost-hardy) In pots and as ground cover. They like sunny, open ground in fertile, well-drained soil.

Peas/*Pisum sativum*

For pea and sage soup, puree soaked peas with cream and fresh sage leaves. Eat raw in salads.

There are many varieties to choose from. Sow in rich well-drained soil from early spring to mid-summer. Provide supports between double rows.

Pumpkin and gourd/
Cucurbita maxima; C. moschata

Use in a soup combined with cream, pepper, cayenne, garlic and dill. Find a recipe for pumpkin pie.

Soak seeds overnight to propagate in pots for planting out in May or June, 1m (3ft) apart in open, sunny and well-manured, draining soil. Water and feed frequently.

Runner beans/*Phaseolus coccineus*

Another crop to try in large pots next to the barbecue. Make a tall 'wigwam' cane support for four plants to give an ample supply.

Sow in a sunny position in mid-spring in fertile, draining soil.

Sorrel/*Rumex acetosa*

Make a delicious green pasta sauce, puree the young leaves, eat raw as an early spring vegetable, or cook like spinach.

Likes acid, cool and moist draining fertile soil. Sow seed in spring or divide plants. Protect with cloches for year round cropping, removing flowers as they appear.

Tomato/*Lycopersicon esculentum*

Grow in pots from seedlings or seeds, next to the barbecue for an instant salad fruit and garnish. Look for cherry tomatoes; they are much easier.

For growing outside, wait until after the last frost. Support constantly, fertilise and water frequently.

Soft fruits

There are so many species and varieties so try your favourites.

Gooseberries/*Ribes uva-crispa* 'Whitesmith'; *R. u.* 'Whinham's Industry'

Gooseberry 'fool' is like nectar from paradise. Trim and puree with cream and sugar, or as a hot sauce on fish.
They are frost-hardy, liking sun or semi-shade in fertile, well-manured moist but draining soil. Plant and prune in the winter and protect young fruits from birds.

Hottentot fig/*Carpobrotus edulis*

An unusual fruiting architectural plant from South Africa. The tangy figs are a taste treat.
Frost tender, they like sun and a moist, draining alkaline soil.

Raspberry/ *Rubus idaeus* 'Malling Jewel' 'Autumn Bliss'

The perfect soft fruit, supplying many vitamins, minerals and fibre. Young leaves make a calming, refreshing tea.
Buy the canes, and plant in a sunny but cool position in well-manured, moist but draining soil, with a post for support. Most varieties fruit on the previous year's growth, autumn-fruiting variety fruits on current growth.

Red currants/*Ribes rubrum* 'Red Lake'

As a jelly these are the best accompaniment to light meats and game and an ingredient with raspberries of 'summer pudding'. Pureed with lemon and honey they make a delicious tart breakfast drink.
Frost hardy they grow in rich and fertile, well-drained soil in a cool position. Thin the new fruit to enhance crop size and flavour.

Wild strawberry/*Fragaria vesca*

The tiny fruits hold more sweetness and flavour than the monster commercials. Wild or alpine strawberries can be bought from good nurseries and can be grown on rocks, around paving or in a container. Frost tender, they like sun or semi-shade and manured well-drained soil.

Top fruit

There are endless varieties to choose. Try for the older varieties, they are often the tastiest. Ask at a good nursery about the right size for your garden; to avoid needing two each time to ensure pollination, there are modern 'family' stocks that are self-pollinating.

Apple/*Malus domestica* 'Egremont Russets' with *M. d.* 'Ribston Pippin'

Cherry/*Prunus avium* 'Stella' (sweet) *Prunus cerasus* 'Morello' (acid)

Pear/*Pyrus communis* 'Doyenne du Comice' with *P. c.* 'Winter Nelis'

Plums, gages, damsons and bullaces/*Prunus domestica* 'Victoria' and *P. d.* 'Cambridge Gage'

In the smaller garden, train them, fan them to frames or walls. A bower made with fruit is inspiring to walk under.

the healing garden

Colours, aroma and sounds affect our health

The art of using plants as a means to restore a sufferer to health is as old as humanity. For our ancestors, surrounded as they were by lush forests, experimenting with plants, observing certain characteristics and ascribing symbolic natures must have been an all-consuming pastime. In more recent times, the sophisticated and developing arts of diagnosing a complaint and applying a remedy have evolved into a technical science based in the analysis of each compound element, with painstaking research into the effects. When you treat an ailment or an emotional problem with a tea made from a flower, root or leaf, massage or apply the oil and fragrance, you are treating herbally.

We might all grow plants in our gardens that we can use medicinally or simply to maintain and enhance our healthy lives. In fact, just tending and having these plants around in the garden may be therapeutic in itself and enough to produce a positive effect. Self-diagnosis is also possible, but never forget, that if symptoms persist you must consult a qualified practitioner.

'Health is our heritage, our right. It is the complete and full union of soul, mind and body. This is no difficult far away ideal to attain, but one so easy and natural that many of us have overlooked it.'   Dr Edward Bach

the healing garden

the flowers

Arnica/*Arnica montana*
A wonderful homoeopathic remedy for shock and trauma, accidents, bruises and muscle strain.
Cultivation – Rhizomatous perennial for the dry border or rock garden. Fully hardy, preferring sun and humus-rich, well-drained soil.

Blackcurrant/*Ribes nigrum*
The leaves are infused as a pleasant tea and the fruits contain a high concentration of Vitamin C. Both prevent infection and strengthen the immune system.
Cultivation – Frost hardy, they need full sun and a fertile, well-drained soil.

Chamomile/*Chamaemelum nobile*
An infusion of the flowers is best known as a calming bedtime drink. Reduces inflammation and fevers.
Cultivation – A ground-covering invasive perennial sown in spring. Likes shade and humus-rich, well-drained soil.

Coriander/*Coriandrum sativum*
A culinary and medicinal herb for good digestion Leaves in salads and with cooked vegetables, the seeds spice bland tastes.
Cultivation – Sow in spring, in a sunny, open and prepared fertile, well-drained soil.

Evening primrose/*Oenothera biennis*
The Flower of Silent Love. Gamma-linolenic acid is the medicinal ingredient of the seeds, important for maintaining hormone balance; used for treating skin complaints like eczema.
Cultivation – A biennial with a powerful evening flower perfume from early summer through autumn. It prefers full sun and almost any well-drained soil.

Feverfew/*Tanacetum parthenium*
Much work has been done with this plant in trials treating migraine. It dilates and relaxes blood vessels and inhibits the release of allergic body chemicals. It has a very bitter taste; an infusion clears catarrh and the sinuses.
Cultivation – A tall, daisy-like perennial herb easily raised from seed. It is hardy, preferring sun and fertile, draining soil.

Garlic/*Allium sativum*
Culinary and medicinal for vitality, strength and energy. An expectorant and antibiotic for respiratory and digestive systems. Also collect Ramsons, the wild species.
Cultivation – Plant in autumn in the warmest wintering spot. Likes full sun and well-manured, well-drained soil. Harvest the bulbs in late summer.

Lemon balm/*Melissa officinalis*
An infusion of the leaves makes a relaxing tea at bedtime. It also helps to bring out colds and flu. The bees love it too.
Cultivation – A favourite tall cottage garden perennial, it grows almost anywhere.

Lemon verbena/*Aloysia triphylla*
An infusion of leaves makes a pleasant tea to aid digestion and reduce fevers.
Cultivation – Propagate under glass, planting out in early summer in a warm sheltered place.

Liquorice/*Glycyrrhiza glabra*
A root herbal remedy for digestion. A common drug derived from it treats peptic ulcers.
Cultivation – A tall Mediterranean perennial pea producing blue flowers in autumn. Needs sun and deep, rich, well-drained soil.

Male fern/*Dryopteris filix-mas*
Included for its shape and soft foliage, because of its toxicity it was once used for warming.
Cultivation – A native fern. Buy or replant as growing from spores is very slow. Fully hardy, it prefers shade and moist soil.

Marigold/*Calendula officinalis*
The oils in Marigold, used as a compress or ointment, are a universal healer, disinfecting and promoting fast healing.
Cultivation – An annual to sow into the prepared borders in spring.

Marjoram/*Origanum majorana; O. vulgare; O. onites*
The culinary and medicinal herb of the oregano family.
O. marjorana or Sweet marjoram is the best known variety for healing.
O. vulgare is the strongest flavoured 'Mediterranean' cooking ingredient.
O. onites is the Marjoram herb for cooking with meat, tomatoes and Provençal dressings.
Cultivation – Deciduous shrubs and perennials, they frost-hardy, preferring sun and alkaline well-drained soil.

Meadow saffron/*Colchicum autumnale*
Included because of the beautiful crocus-like flowers used to treat arthritis and gout. It has been used in genetic research and for cancer treatment. An homoeopathic gem.
Cultivation – An autumn flowering bulb, corms planted in late summer, in rich well-drained soil.

Opium poppy/*Papaver somniferum*
Temperate climates are rarely hot enough for the plants to mature and produce the drug morphine, one of the best known of all painkillers. The flowers, however, are beautiful.
Cultivation – Self-seeding annuals or propagated by seed in autumn or spring. They prefer sun and moist, well-drained soil.

Peppermint/*Mentha* x *piperita*

The Flower of Refreshment. A magnificent culinary and medicinal herb. As a tonic, a warming tea of the leaves relieves winter ailments. Fresh crushed leaves added to a lotion are good for general aches and pains; it is extensively used as an antiseptic and a flavouring.

Cultivation – A native, it is quite invasive and needs to be controlled, in a container perhaps. It prefers semi-shade in moist, humus-rich soil.

Rose/*Rosa* x *damascena;* R. x *centifolia*

The old fashioned roses are rather special to aromatherapy and perfumery. Leaves and petals infused have many other uses as well, including bringing down fevers, clearing toxins and enhancing immunity. The hips are also used but require much careful handling to remove the hairs within.

Cultivation – Deciduous and evergreen shrubs, preferring full sun and fertile well-drained soil. They may need training and supporting.

Rosemary/*Rosmarinus officinalis*

A culinary and medicinal herb used as a meat condiment and as a stimulating and antiseptic infusion and aromatherapy oil.

Cultivation – An evergreen shrub, best cultivated from cuttings or young plants in late summer. Frost hardy but needing protection and a warm spot in sun and well-drained soil.

St John's Wort/*Hypericum perforatum*

A personal favourite, it is the 'Flower of Light'. Its homoeopathic remedy is used to 'lighten us'.

Cultivation – A beautiful spreading perennial of the open woods and moist grasslands, with golden yellow flowers. Some varieties are perfect ground cover for the border.

Skullcap/*Scutellaria lateriflora*

The Flower of Relaxation. Traditionally an infusion of leaves and flowers and homoeopathic solution is used to treat every kind of nervous complaint. It is particularly strengthening during stress.

Cultivation – A perennial of marginal wet places, it thrives in almost any moist soil.

Valerian/*Valeriana officinalis*

The root is where the medicinal sedative properties are found. A cold 24-hour infusion of the crushed root is effective for stress and anxiety.

Cultivation – A temperate perennial. Plant young seedlings in spring, in full sun and almost any fertile draining soil.

Witch hazel/*Hamamelis virginiana*

A favourite homoeopathic and tincture remedy for all types of skin complaints requiring astringent or cleansing.

Cultivation – A deciduous shrub tree, having beautiful autumn colour and flowers in winter. Needs deep fertile, peaty soil in sun or semi-shade.

Yarrow/*Achillea millifolium*

An infusion of the root and crushed leaves traditionally used to stop bleeding, as a vaginal douche, an eyebath, or for good digestion.

Cultivation – A native perennial with white flowers through summer. Will self-seed, sometimes too easily.

Yellow gentian/*Gentiana in tea*

A bitter root herbal remedy acting as a stimulant to digestive juices and as a cleansing and a strengthening agent.

Cultivation – A tall European perennial. Sow seed in warm partial shade and moist soil.

the healing garden
the art of holistic healing

We are beginning to understand that there is a deeply holistic nature to all things. Each and every living organism has its place in the order of Nature, each has its role to play. In the case of plants, their chemical exchange with their environment is most important. Plants are favoured by us for their colour and shape, their perfume or their food value, but for the plants life is about the interdependent survival and success of their seed – a seed which will fit precisely its ecological niche, whose success will depend on the parent plant's correct absorption and secretion of the tiniest trace elements. Moment by moment this interaction with gases, with microbial bacteria, with sunlight and enriched water, is all an intricate part of an exchange of resources needed for life itself.

The more we learn about plant life, the more realise how useful they are to us, how much of their chemistry is also ours and therefore likely to be a necessary constituent part of our own healthy living.

Lavender/*Lavandula officinalis*

One of the most popular scented and healing shrubs of all time. From the ancient Greeks, Romans and probably long before that, we have used its aroma and its lightening effects. In the sixteenth century it was thought to be 'especially good for all of the griefs and pains of the head and heart. To be used in maladies of the brain due to coldness, for comfort of the stomach and obstructions of the liver and spleen.' Lavender has been used to treat a range of ailments including; anxiety and tension, arthritis and rheumatism, indigestion, flatulence and poor appetite, insect bites and stings, insomnia, muscular aches and pains, nausea and nervous complaints.

The leaves can be harvested at any time, but flowers and stems should be taken as soon as the flowers open. You can dry the leaves by hanging small bunches upside down with a paper bag over the flower heads. Lavender can be taken as a tea, a tincture or a pure oil. Use fresh or dried leaves, but some efficacy is lost in drying. You might simply put a small bunch of flowered stems under the hot tap when you run a bath. The fragrance and the calming and uplifting effect is undeniable.

Growing Lavender is simple. To propagate it, sow in late summer or root 10–20cm (4–8in) stem cuttings in spring or summer. Thin or transplant to about a 30–45cm (12–18in) apart to make a hedge-like row. Lavender likes a lot of sun and, although it will grow almost anywhere, it prefers a well-drained sandy soil. Prune the plants in spring to maintain a compact growth. Look out for the large flower-heads of 'french' lavender.

Home herbal preparations

• **Compress** – Lint, cotton wool or a flannel is dipped into a herbal tea or infusion and applied externally, hot or more usually cold, for abrasions, bruises, aches and pains.

• **Infusion** – A tea. Cover the herb leaves or flowers with boiling water for a few minutes. The properties are transferred to the water and the liquid is strained before using.

• **Oil** – The herb leaves or flowers are infused for a month or so in a good oil: sweet almond or grapeseed, with a very small amount of vinegar, in a warm place. Strain and discard the herbs to use as a massage oil or burning aroma.

• **Ointment** – Crushed herbs or flowers are added to melted petroleum jelly which is then simmered gently for 20–30 minutes. Strain out the solids before using externally.

• **Tincture** – Crushed dried herbs or flowers are preserved in alcohol with a little added water. Brandy, gin or vodka are suitable. Leave for about 14 days, shaking daily, then press out the liquid to store. Dilute with water to imbibe.

• **Syrup** – Add sugar to a herbal infusion and simmer until syrupy. This is pleasant to take for children's minor ailments.

WARNING – Do not try to treat ailments that you do not understand. Seek professional advice first. If the symptoms persist, consult a qualified practitioner.

inspirational
gardens

The gardens featured on the following pages provide a
wealth of inspirational ideas for the creation of your
own garden sanctuary. Each garden works in harmony
with the environment, employing an aesthetic quality,
that is more than just an appreciation of beauty. The
viewer's imagination is stimulated by the artful
creation and use of innovative ideas expressed within
each garden. Not just interesting or beautiful to look
at, but more – an experience that teaches and opens
the mind to new ideas.

'We think of a time to work and a time to play, and
complain of a lack of time for as much play or rest as
we want. In all primitive communities I have visited,
however, work time merges into play time, or better, no
one really distinguishes between the two.'

Elman R. Service – Anthropologist

the forest garden

an urban wildlife sanctuary?

In his forest garden in Shropshire, Robert Hart believes that any plant organism in a positive state of health will encourage wildlife and at the same time resist pests and diseases. Even the Bullfinch from the Apple tree, he says! This is the result of an immune system which nature provides to all living organisms. Left in a natural state nature, constantly seeks an equilibrium of health and balance, and aiming to work this miracle well is how best to encourage wildlife into the garden, as well as eradicating pests and diseases. The forest garden is a miniature reproduction of the self-maintaining ecosystem of the natural forest. It consists entirely of fruit and nut trees and bushes, perennial and self-seeding vegetables, and culinary and medicinal herbs.

a forest *in miniature*

Robert's garden took only two years to establish and now, because of the choice of plants, it is self-perpetuating, self-fertilising, self-watering, self-mulching, self-pollinating and self-healing. The only work required is regular pruning to control plants that seek to encroach, and mulching with compost once a year in autumn when the herbaceous plants have died back.

What better choice of garden to celebrate as a sanctuary than the form that nature intended? One of the best ways to repair any damage to nature is to emulate her, and so the forest garden acts as a perfect example of the new aesthetic.

Plants and trees that are attractive to birds, insects and butterflies

Barberry	*Berberis* x *tsenophylla*
Barberry variety	*Caryopteris* x *clandonensis*
Bird cherry	*Prunus padus*
Butterfly bushes	*Buddleja davidii*
Cornflower	*Centaurea cyanus*
Cotoneaster	*Cotoneaster horizontalis*
Crab apple	*Malus*
Dogwood	*Cornus sanguinea*
Elder	*Sambucus nigra*
Evening primrose	*Oenothera biennis*
Firethorn	*Pyracantha*
Hebes	*Hebes*
Heliotrope	*Heliotropium*
Hemp agrimony	*Eupatorium cannabinum*
Holly	*Ilex aquifolium*
Honeysuckle	*Lonicera periclymenum*
Hyssop	*Hyssopus officinalis*
Lavender	*Lavandula*
Michaelmas daisies	*Aster novi-belgii*
Rowan	*Sorbus aucuparia*
Sedum	*Sedum*
Soapwort	*Saponaria officinalis*
Spindle	*Euonymus europaeus*
Spiraea	*Spiraea japonica*
Sunflower	*Helianthus annuus*
Teasel	*Dipsacus fullonum*
Thyme	*Thymus*
Verbena	*Verbena bonariensis*
Viburnum	*Viburnum tinus and V. opulus*
Yew	*Taxus baccata*

Chalice well – Glastonbury

a real sacred garden

The Chalice Well, in the shadow of the Tor at Glastonbury, has been revered as sacred for as long as anyone can remember. Ynis Witrin, the Glassy Isle, was once an island rising high above a marshy inland sea. The first visitors found a remarkable natural phenomenon of a coloured white spring coming out of the rocks within a few feet of a coloured red spring. Their sources are now thought to be quite different, the waters travelling for many miles underground, picking up the coloured minerals and nutrients that make them so distinctive. The iron-rich red and calcium carbonate white waters were believed to represent the earth's female blood and the male semen. This is what predates and underlies the founding of Glastonbury as the sacred site that has drawn pilgrims for centuries.

No one seems to be clear exactly when the sanctuary gardens were first built as they have been constantly closed, built over and re-dedicated throughout the years, according to the prevailing beliefs and taboos. Today, it is one of the really true sacred gardens in existence.

Since the early 1960s, however, the gardens of the 'Blood Spring' have been laid out with a succession of pools which carry the well water, running at a 4,500 l (1,000 gal) an hour, through a series of terraces along the gentle hillside slope. These pools incorporate the iron-red coated ceremonial and bathing ponds and several beautifully laid out gardens for meditation and peaceful contemplation. In recent years the gardens have become a tourist attraction providing the funds to develop and further beautify extensive borders and plantings alongside grassy, bulb-strewn banks under shading trees. It is an idyllic spot, especially as a haven from the now busy main road nearby and a wonderful place to relax and refresh after the arduous and invigorating climb up the Tor.

The well head is now buried, but a stone well structure within the garden is the beautiful focus of pilgrimage. The well shaft is adorned with a symbolic cover depicting two interlinked circles representing the merging of the worlds of spirit and matter. This *Vesica Piscis*, the oval shape formed by two overlapping circles, is a powerful symbol (shown above) of the creation and regeneration of forms in the natural world and, has come to be adopted by many modern pilgrims as an evocation of a new belief in the sanctity of nature. There is an idea that for global peace and harmony, the red and white spring waters should now be combined. The gardens that channel the red spring are now the place of many regular ceremonies and prayers to send this thought out with the water.

A practical idea

Recreate the *Vesica Piscis* symbol in the garden by combining it with your water feature, to align yourself with, and support those prayers.

Jarman's garden

driftwood at its best

The late film director and writer Derek Jarman created a stunning garden, which lies on the shingle beach at Dungeness on the English south coast, is something special and refreshingly different. 'Gertrude Jekyll would turn in her grave!' You can however, see instantly how it is made. Walks to the sea in the morning yielded wonderful, unusually shaped, weathered, holed stones and pieces of odd driftwood.

All these items, once accumulated, end up shambolically combined to produce sculptures that are wholly natural and unique, objects that arrive, worn and shaped by their journey.

Once Derek began visiting nurseries, the stock of varied local plants in the garden increased, but remains mixed with the wild and indigenous sea kale or gorse, all growing out from between the shingle and flint. There are no fences surrounding the garden, so rather like the Japanese temple gardens, the idea prevails of 'blurring the edges' between the garden and the rest of the beach. The garden just fades out, giving way to the mottled and austere humps and occasionally green dimples of the stony marsh.

The garden is ecologically sound, sitting within a designated 'Site of Special Scientific Interest', the rules of which restrict the plants that can be grown. Derek was criticised by some people because he introduced local flowers, but these are still so-called weeds that would be growing there

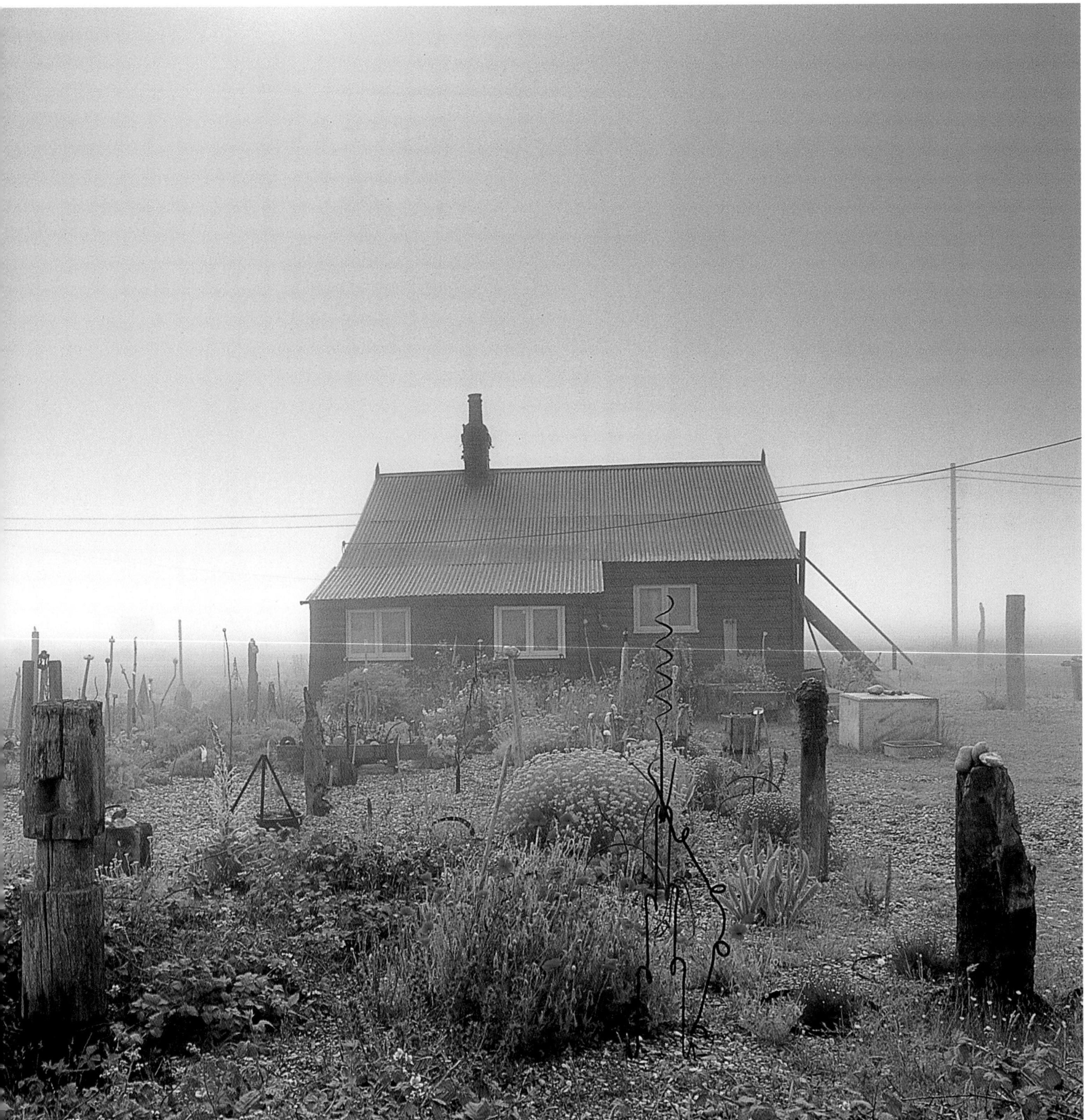

but for the effect of the wind. They
are planted in the lee of little shingle
mounds and behind the gorse bushes
for shelter. White campion, mallow,
rest-harrow and scabious, the odd rather
spindly rose and some elder close to the
wooden fisherman's cottage, all make a
little paradise in the heart of wilderness
or vice versa.

Derek's garden is special, for in it
are treasured the old and the worn, the
found and the sentimental: a personal
emporium of memories and a way of
preserving the flotsam of life. Old tools,
a trowel handle, or a rusty fork that has
seen many years of loving use, become
sculptures, features that sometimes lie
almost hidden beneath a plant
arrangement. All seem to embody the
magic of going for a walk and finding
a unique, 'right' piece of wood or an
oddly shaped branch or log. Decorating
the sculptures are special stones, whose
weathered shape can never be recreated
except by nature and her enduring and
ever-changing forces, add another
dimension.

A practical idea

Next time you go for a walk, pick up that knurled and odd shaped-log or sea-worn rock. Bring it home and find it a place of pride in the garden.

'What would the world be, once bereft
of wet and of wildness? Let them be left.
Oh let them be left, wildness and wet,
long live the weeds and the wilderness yet'

Gerard Manley Hopkins

Hannah Peschar sculpture garden

inspiring lofty imagination

the *joy of art and nature together*

A prominent tradition throughout the history of sacred gardens is the commissioning of art to inspire and encourage praise and celebration. Alongside statues of the deities and divine characters, symbolic and meaningful objects, placed with great care and accuracy, are intended to focus the attention and inspire one's imagination.

In attempting to create our modern idea of the sacred in the garden, art and *objets d'art* can play an important role. It is probably true to say that for most of us garden sculpture is something we think about but find it difficult to know what to do about: which materials and forms to choose. In our sacred garden, however, the choice is a little easier if we imagine the kinds of images that provoke our thoughts. Think about images that are meaningful to you, and add the concept of complementing nature, using it as a backdrop or as part of the piece and; then, the possibilities become easier to grasp.

A wonderful example exists at Hannah Peschar's Sculpture Garden in the midst of the last wooded areas south of London, at Ockley in Surrey. With sculptures from around 45 artists, the 4ha (10-acre) garden is full of wonderfully imaginative romance and surprise. Winding paths and moss-covered steps, reflecting pools and bubbling streams blend perfectly with sculptures in hollows and shaded clearings, The garden features appear like naturally occurring, living works of art, when gazing over the weir from a wooden Monet-like bridge or stepping gingerly across a water walkway surrounded by gunneras and lingularias, the next vista, of which there are many, cleverly manipulates light and shade to meet yet another intriguing and wild figure.

Art and nature are of the same order, facets of the same jewel: a partly hidden shape, an angle, a subtle sparkle of light. When the artist's dream, and its setting are chosen well, each complements and highlights the other. The border blurs between the two, and a kinetic excitement, an expectant magic appears to set our imagination free.

Just like nature, the wind blows and you are a little unsettled. There is time to dream, sitting on a cosy greenwood seat, before the more sensual sculptural delights of the garden appear from every hidden corner of the garden: 'Not a garden for the faint-hearted', Hannah said. And it's true. The garden has managed to combine successfully surprise and sensual effrontery, providing an exquisite experience of nature, a heartfelt fantasy, with a sense of anticipation as life's drama unfolds.

If there ever was a garden designed to inspire divine imagination, this is it. Although this is a large garden, the real magic is in the tiny detail, a visual texture cliché of weeping leaves over the water, a light reflecting mirror image, a single plant raised on a mound to give it presence. And, hidden just behind the holly bush, what mystery may soon be revealed. . .

A practical idea

As with the driftwood garden, garden sculpture can include any object that holds significance for you. Give the garden your own personal touch by incorporating a piece of art that has a personal significance to you. Try painting an area of the garden, or creating your own garden sculpture using natural materials. Create an impact by partially obscuring sculpture with plants, or placing objects in remote parts of the garden to increase the element of surprise when they are revealed.

ancient traditions

The site of the earliest known gardens, known as the 'cradle of civilisation', lies between what are now the deserts of north Africa and the valleys of the Euphrates river. Newly settled communities first made gardens which they surrounded by walled protection from the desert winds. They grew fruit and nuts, herbs and medicinal plants.

While cultivating plants simply for beauty implies a degree of afforded luxury not known to those poor first farmers, trees and flowers happily fulfil a dual role, and so the useful trees, herbs and medicinal plants, laid out in a symmetry for ease of irrigation and cultivation, at once assumed a decorative character. These gardens emphasise the contrasts between two separate worlds: the outer where nature is awe-inspiringly all-powerful and unpredictable, and the inner, a sanctuary where our plant food and medicine can be protected from that which is beyond our control. For us, in shade and shelter with water at hand, the garden becomes a place to feel safe, to refresh the spirit – a haven offering growth and nourishment.

Through the chain of evolution, stretching back perhaps 10,000 years, ornamental and sanctuary gardens have been designed, with many plants assuming symbolic or religious meaning. They developed from humble beginnings into the fountain of aesthetic pleasure that we now understand to be a true craft and a treasured art form – gardening.

the Persian garden

water, the stuff of life

Water was the most precious commodity, so the desert oasis was the inspiration for the Persian garden design, and flourishing examples of this style can still be found in Spain and India. Sparkling, splashing and rippling water, shading fruit and nut trees, many coloured flowers and geometric-patterned tile mosaics are all features that have been adapted to a variety of climatic conditions. A narrow linear channel, facing brightly coloured and patterned tiles, is lined with starkly geometric pines and cypress. Tiny sparing fountains help the cooling waters fill the air and flow through the whole garden area. According to the Koran, the holy book of Islam, a river, the source of all life and purifier of everything, went out of Eden to water the gardens. There it parted and became four riverheads: the water, the wine, the milk and the honey. This pattern of the four rivers is repeated in every Persian-influenced garden.

Havens of order in the chaotic world, oases in every sense, these gardens are often very formal in design, highly structured and symmetrically square to express the spiritual conformity of the universe. If water is not available then it is represented by low myrtle hedges or pattered stones that sparkle in the sunlight. Blue and gold tiles reflect and imitate the sun, water and sky.

the *walled garden*

It is possible that the Persian garden derives precisely from those original walled and irrigated orchards: fruit and nut trees planted out in lines with narrow channels of sparingly distributed water to feed them; the nomad's dream of a cool, shaded Eden with running water, fruit and scent inside protecting walls. Sunken square beds grew red roses, the special favourite of the Prophet Muhammad. Scented climbing jasmines, medicinal and culinary herbs, blue lilies and bulbs, gold irises and red tulips. According to the instruction of the Koran, to imitate the true terrestrial paradise, the riverhead of wine was certain to be represented by grapevines planted beneath the shading trees.

In hot climates receptions, daily prayers and meals were held under the shade of the spreading trees. Popular features and decorations included majestic tiled and mosaic arched entrances and gateways. The minaret roofed platform for viewing the moon and stars, called the gazebo, has become an icon for the Persian style. Its cool tiled floor scattered with embroidered cushions and carpets depict the garden elements of water, flowers, trees and birds.

Into the middle ages, Islamic gardeners became renowned as botanists, collectors and breeders of rare and new varieties. It was usual not to plant in massed drifts as in modern gardens, but to plant singly, making a feature of the individual, allowing it to spread alone, perhaps from a clover lawn.

It is said that Persian and Islamic garden art reached its peak with the Mogal emperors of India and Kashmir. Our modern evidence of this exists only in the miniature period paintings that have survived. However, these depict grand designs, strictly following dictated tradition and built into the plains and mountain landscapes. Crops and orchards, wild roses and violet irises, fields of sparkling saffron, all fed by the four riverheads of the Koran. The pride and untold riches of emperors was celebrated by their apparent power over nature to make the deserts bloom.

Egypt and beyond

sacred beginnings

In Egyptian ceremonial art of around 2,800 BC, stylised versions of trees, flowers and leaves, hint at an aesthetic as well as material appreciation of the beauty of plants. The palm, with its many fruits, became deified as a symbol of fertility in the temple gardens. The ubiquitous papyrus, utilised for everything from paper to building, was depicted as having magical qualities, a symbol of resurrection in tomb paintings and funeral bouquets. The lotus, with both its flower and leaf considered sacred, has been used by Egyptian, Minion and Assyrian artisans alike. These water-loving plants depended on irrigation, and this is one of the most prominent symbols of our power over nature, their blossoming and fruiting the proof of our potency.

The famous Sumerian poem, 'The Epic of Gilgamesh' in the second millennium BC, tells of the groves of the plain, where a fabled king planted date palms and tamarisk in the courtyard of his palace. The fruit was grown to be used as offerings. A contemporary Babylonian text proclaimed, 'I planted a pure orchard for the goddess and established fruit deliveries as regular offerings'. A 'Temptation Seal' from this period shows a subject akin to Adam and Eve and confirms the idea of the sacred nature of trees. Two horned figures, a male and female, sit either side of a central, sacred Tree of Knowledge, while a predatory serpent lurks behind.

the *garden of Eden*

The first actual records of sacred gardens are found at the time of the return of the Assyrians at the beginning of the tenth century BC. Groves of trees, planted around their temples, had a special significance. Palm trees, pines and pomegranates assumed symbolic personalities and special rites took place 'under every garden tree'.

An Assyrian narrative bas-relief depicts a vivid landscape of natural mountains and rivers, marshes, parks and gardens alive with luxuriant flowers, trees and fruit. It is easy to see why later chroniclers placed the Garden of Eden in these regions.

The few traces actually found of palace or temple gardens show courtyards for retreat and meditation where palms, pines and fruit trees were laid out in geometric patterns. Water was raised to lush roof gardens that resembled the pyramid ziggurats. These artificial mountain designs were the beginnings of the recognisable ramped or stepped tree-lined access such as that later employed by Nebuchadnezzar II for the famous Hanging Gardens of Babylon overlooking the Euphrates river.

A practical idea

Murals or hieroglyphs look great painted onto the walls. Even specially waterproofed picture frames that can be hung on an upright surface. We are so concerned with plants and soil and more conventional things, but for the garden to be a proper extension of the house, like another room, why not incorporate pictures, decorated or coloured walls, mirrors and tiles?

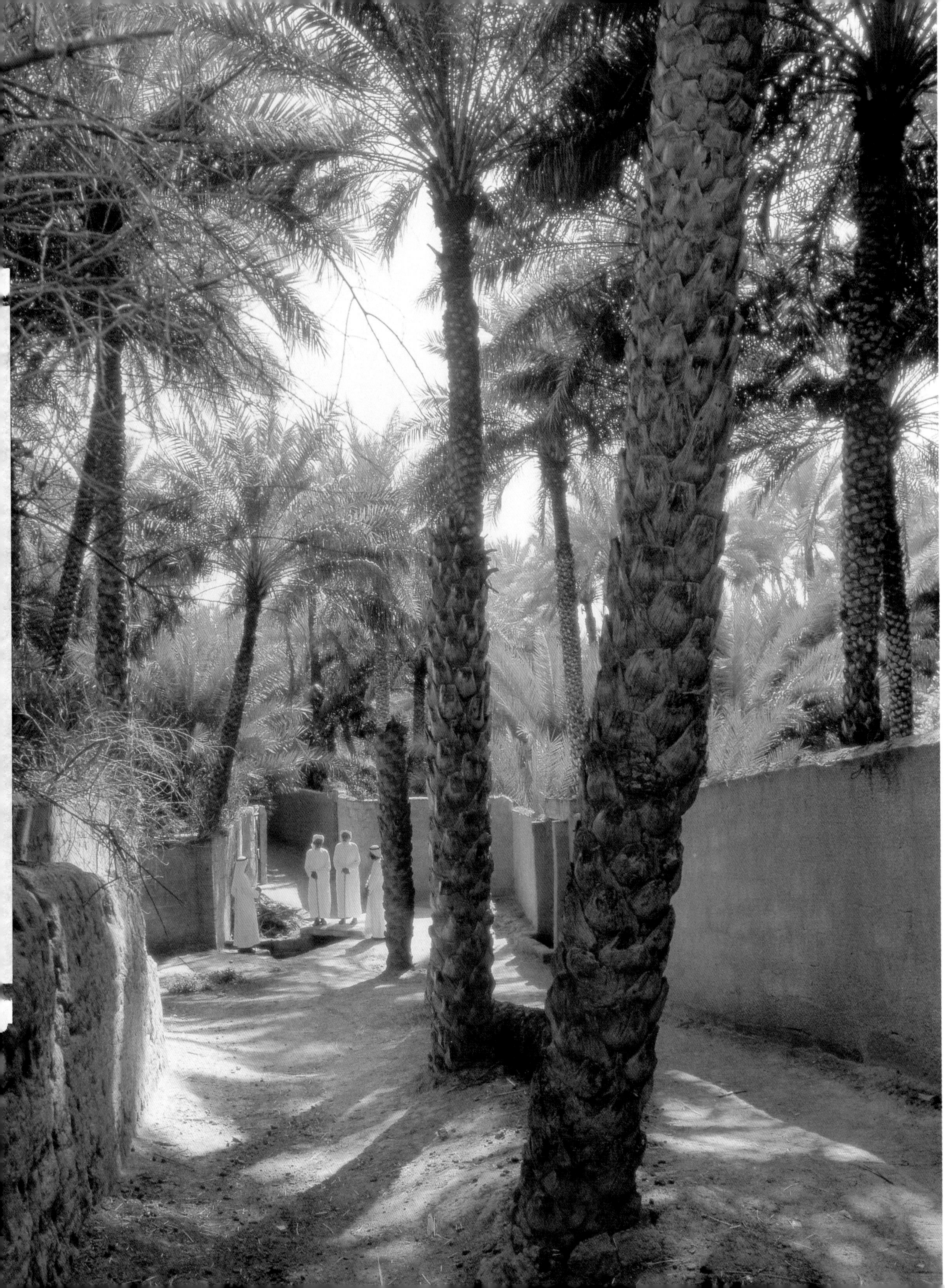

the Persian garden

water, the stuff of life

Water was the most precious commodity, so the desert oasis was the inspiration for the Persian garden design, and flourishing examples of this style can still be found in Spain and India. Sparkling, splashing and rippling water, shading fruit and nut trees, many coloured flowers and geometric-patterned tile mosaics are all features that have been adapted to a variety of climatic conditions. A narrow linear channel, facing brightly coloured and patterned tiles, is lined with starkly geometric pines and cypress. Tiny sparing fountains help the cooling waters fill the air and flow through the whole garden area. According to the Koran, the holy book of Islam, a river, the source of all life and purifier of everything, went out of Eden to water the gardens. There it parted and became four riverheads: the water, the wine, the milk and the honey. This pattern of the four rivers is repeated in every Persian-influenced garden.

Havens of order in the chaotic world, oases in every sense, these gardens are often very formal in design, highly structured and symmetrically square to express the spiritual conformity of the universe. If water is not available then it is represented by low myrtle hedges or pattered stones that sparkle in the sunlight. Blue and gold tiles reflect and imitate the sun, water and sky.

the *walled garden*

It is possible that the Persian garden derives precisely from those original walled and irrigated orchards: fruit and nut trees planted out in lines with narrow channels of sparingly distributed water to feed them; the nomad's dream of a cool, shaded Eden with running water, fruit and scent inside protecting walls. Sunken square beds grew red roses, the special favourite of the Prophet Muhammad. Scented climbing jasmines, medicinal and culinary herbs, blue lilies and bulbs, gold irises and red tulips. According to the instruction of the Koran, to imitate the true terrestrial paradise, the riverhead of wine was certain to be represented by grapevines planted beneath the shading trees.

In hot climates receptions, daily prayers and meals were held under the shade of the spreading trees. Popular features and decorations included majestic tiled and mosaic arched entrances and gateways. The minaret roofed platform for viewing the moon and stars, called the gazebo, has become an icon for the Persian style. Its cool tiled floor scattered with embroidered cushions and carpets depict the garden elements of water, flowers, trees and birds.

Into the middle ages, Islamic gardeners became renowned as botanists, collectors and breeders of rare and new varieties. It was usual not to plant in massed drifts as in modern gardens, but to plant singly, making a feature of the individual, allowing it to spread alone, perhaps from a clover lawn.

It is said that Persian and Islamic garden art reached its peak with the Mogal emperors of India and Kashmir. Our modern evidence of this exists only in the miniature period paintings that have survived. However, these depict grand designs, strictly following dictated tradition and built into the plains and mountain landscapes. Crops and orchards, wild roses and violet irises, fields of sparkling saffron, all fed by the four riverheads of the Koran. The pride and untold riches of emperors was celebrated by their apparent power over nature to make the deserts bloom.

A practical idea

In the Persian garden design the most important element is the use of precious water: narrow channels, tiny meandering enclosed canals. When we think of water in the garden, it is usually as a pond or fountain, but sculptured and shaped water channels within or at the front of the border or alongside a path add another dimension. Of course these should be safe and need only be very shallow.

Zen and Japanese garden
The art of understatement

The art of Zen and Japanese gardening is based upon understatement. Rock, water, sand and moss, meticulously pruned trees and fragrant flowers, all convey a natural harmony. In a tradition that has remained unchanged since the Buddha taught in the monasteries and gardens of the Ganges valleys more than 2,400 years ago, these gardens are plain yet beautiful. Their whole purpose is to create a natural and calm atmosphere to separate the viewer from the distractions and tensions of the everyday world. In the temples, flowers are considered the most suitable offerings. Across Asia, from Japan and Laos to Sri Lanka and Tibet, people prepare their flower offerings, collected at precisely prescribed times of the day or month to display in the temples, or at home. Old-style tea roses, frangipani flowers, varieties of white and pink jasmine, are each arranged on green leaves, presented at the feet of the Buddha to bring merit and praise.

Culturally, the garden is seen traditionally as a place of meditation, rooted in an appreciation for the natural environment. Miniature representations of mountains and forests or islands in the sea act as a focus for the imagination. They often employ intriguing guile to lead the viewer to a scene of tranquillity and inspiring beauty. A rough path, where you are compelled to watch your

feet, leads to a level platform, where only on reaching it are your eyes free to look up and take in the view. A monk gardener might tell you that he knows little of western gardens, but one difference is that in his garden, the whole idea is to blur the boundary between the garden and the environment beyond: With symbolism and imagery composed to derive the most profound and simple pleasure, these gardens are not in any sense wild but are planned to the smallest detail for every mood or occasion.

four *styles of garden*

In Japan, four main styles have come to be most popular. The Dry Rock, has shaped boulders covered in moss set in combed sand or gravel, appearing like tiny islands in the sea. In the Water Garden are mini falls and streams and dripping sculptures. The Literary Men's garden is a small and tranquil space with seating to encourage discussion or reading, its modern counterpart being the tiny urban courtyard with perhaps a wall-painted landscape and one shapely container tree. Finally, the Tea garden is planned to serve as a path or approach, a soothing and restraining experience leading to the tea ceremony. Little twisting paths and stepping stones, like tiny rivers, slow your pace and remove you for a time from the everyday world, to contemplate the essence of life.

A practical idea

Try making a dry garden. It need only be a small area of shingle which you can comb with a rake. Place some boulders in the centre with some container or rock plants, symbolising a forest on a mountain.

native American

a myth of paradise

The Native Americans were nomadic hunter-gatherers who viewed nature as their temple and provider. Although they do not have a tradition of static gardens, their contribution is counted here however, because of the Emergence Myth of Paradise, which they share with some of the people of the Pacific islands. This myth centres around the symbolism of Mother Earth; how within it, we humans have evolved from the fertile source, the Womb of Paradise, which contains the potency of all life. We emerge through the various stages of life as nature spirits, the plains of existence that underlie the physical world. Similar traditions can be found in many belief systems, but perhaps the best expression is the Native American Medicine Wheel, a metaphor for our journey through developing life. The Medicine Wheel is depicted as a circle of stones representing life stages, which are often described as particular animal and plant characters. These characters are each sentient beings requiring respect: the plants, trees, animals, earth and sky. Every element, every spirit character, every step along the way, has a gift for us, its Medicine.

The native American compass or medicine wheel

Sky Home of the stars and sun, whose light gives the spark to life.
Earth The giver of birth and nourishment to the light.
East The Eagle and male principle. Detached and seeing from afar. Brings renewal and illumination.
South The Koyote, and childlike trust and innocence. Travelling through the day, helping all to grow, chlorophyll green of the plants, red life blood.
West The Bear and female principle. Spirit of intuition and introspection. The place of endings and the hidden and secret night.
North The Buffalo wisdom-keeper. Provider of all material for living: water, food and shelter. The place of thanksgiving.

A practical idea

The medicine wheel

An essential element of creating a sacred space in the Native American tradition is to lay out an actual stone Medicine Wheel. In the pattern of the Natural Calendar, four stones are placed at each of the cardinal points, with two stones in the middle to represent 'above' and 'below'; the sky and earth. An aid to prayer and meditation is to pass from each stone, picking it up, looking at it carefully and invoking or 'calling in' all of the spirit of its direction to come and assist. Starting with the sky, then followed by the earth, then the directions east, south, west and north. These prayers come from the heart and thank the spirits for all their help today, inviting them to come and assist with the tasks at hand, to encourage and preserve our family of living things. Smoke is offered to each direction; a reminder of the breath of life, it carries the prayers. A smoking candle, incense stick or in the way of the Native Americans , a smouldering sage brush or ceremonial pipe, to produce the smoke.

Begin with these six stones adding more stones to the circle as your knowledge develops. Tread carefully, when laying out or at each prayer. Ask for permission or the sanction of each of these directions. Any sense of reluctance or encouragement is noted. At the moment of your request or invocation, a bird may begin to sing or the sun appear from behind a cloud.

feng shui

smooth and free flowing energy

More than 5,000 years old, invented so long before urban sprawls and unnatural barriers, the art of Feng Shui derives from the Taoist belief system of ancient China. Taoist belief states that everything in the world and universe contains an all-pervading life-giving force known as 'Chi'. The tradition says that this chi must flow free and smoothly in order for all things to be energised by it or given healthy life. The chi is a mixture of two forms, a positive and negative, yang and yin. The yang energy form is expansive like light or heat and the yin is introverted, the shadows and dark, the coldness of night. For true health and harmony, everything on Earth requires a balance of these two elements, but sometimes the balance is upset. Feng Shui practice aims to balance these opposing elements by encouraging their free flow and uninterrupted passage. In this way all elements are enriched and harmonised.

Feng Shui, which means in Chinese, 'wind and water', employs specially

the *flow of wind and water*

prescribed techniques to make this fast flowing chi energy stay longer, lingering where more of its harmonising effect is needed. The chi will work at its best when it has absorbed equally the attributes of the fundamental elements of earth, metal, water, wood and fire. It may require re-routing to avoid an obstacle in its flow or a discordant object may need particular attention. The chi energy likes to flow in smooth sweeps, straight edges or sharp corners will not help it. Dark corners and dead ends will trap and stagnate it. Disharmonious edges or unproductive shapes can be remedied or improved by lightening the area with reflective materials like water or the placement of a smoothing shape or object. Sometimes the chi will be funnelled into a narrow passage, passing too fast to provide the correct enrichment. Here it is important to slow it by introducing a curve like a winding path or placing an object in the flow to bend the energy and cause it to linger. Altering the flow of a straight garden path may be quite simple, perhaps by placing a plant or sounding chimes in the flow.

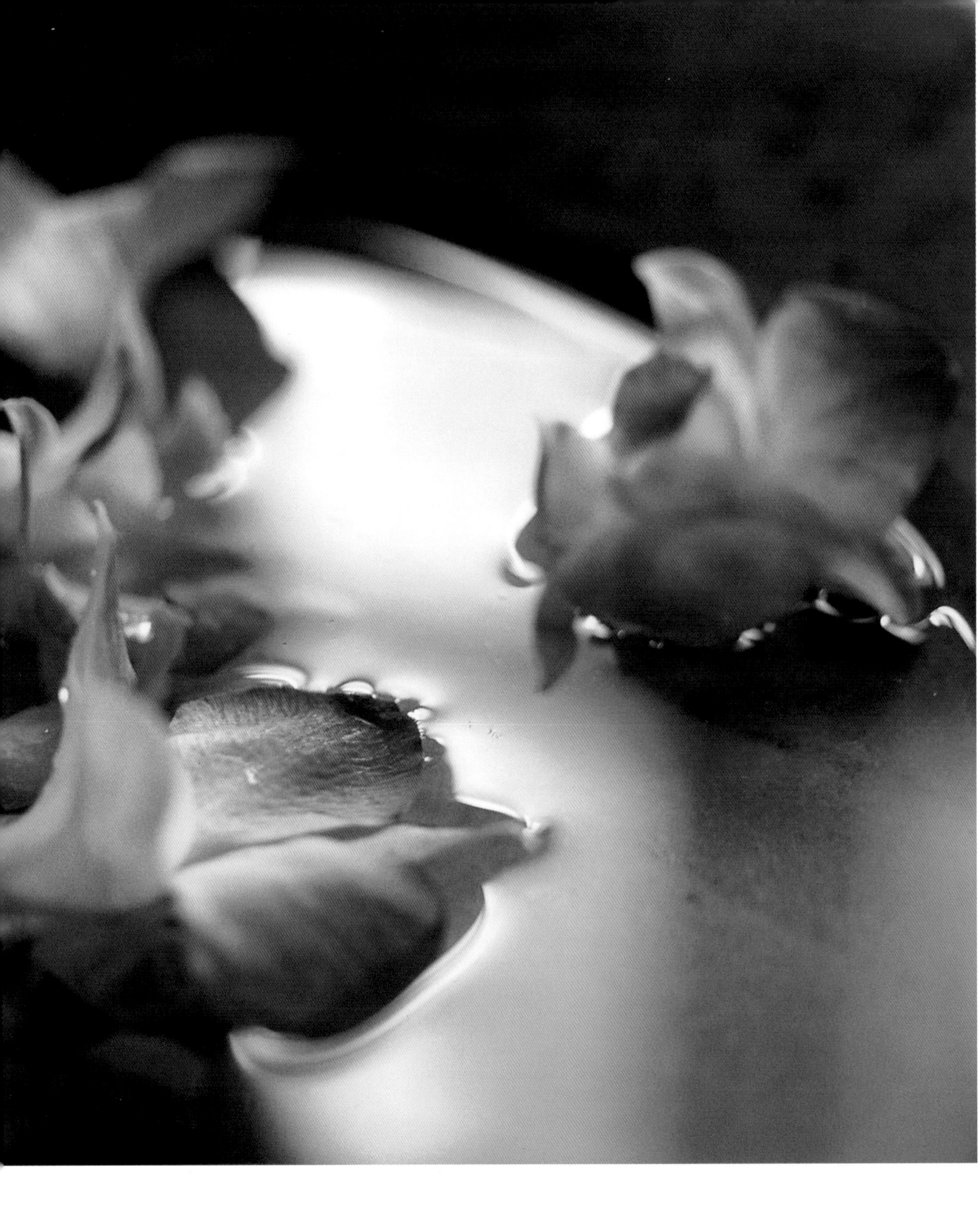

renaissance

the grand style

In the sixteenth century people in Europe began to travel as never before, bringing home the fruits and wealth of other cultures. They accumulated the riches and the consequent knowledge by experimenting and pushing the barriers of the arts and sciences beyond anything that had been dreamt of. For the first time, people began to really believe, that God gave man dominion over nature. Their imagination and their power was then put it into practice and given free reign to create almost anything by man's labour alone. Wealthy merchants, princes and high priests began to display and flaunt this power in the homes they built, in the architecture of their grand estates and the gardens that surrounded them. Medieval scholars deduced that the Garden of Eden must still exist. By the mid-1500s when much of the earth had been explored yet the Garden of Eden remained undiscovered, they decided instead that it should be recreated by gathering together its elements and designing the most grand exhibits to contain of all of the evidence of God's handiwork. Allied to the new scientific expressions of Platonic geometry, of high alchemy and the burgeoning arts of botany and chemistry, it became something of a fashion for the rich and powerful to spare no expense in recreating their idea of an ordered and mechanical universe. The resulting fantastic gardens were opulent and extravagant in the extreme.

In Italy and later in France, huge projects were undertaken to order and

rule the landscape around villas and chateaux. Artificial lake structures with classical pillars, statues and architectural fantasy grottoes, pavilions and majestic fountains were approached through immense geometrically precise avenues of topiaried trees. Many gardens, like those of the palace of Versailles, commissioned by Louis XIV to exemplify his power and imagined relationship to the sun and universe, took over 50 years to complete. So grand was the scale and concept that the theories of gardening expressed there have, ever since, greatly influenced other designers in Europe, Russia, America and even China. The keynotes of formality and ultimate power over nature, established a tradition that has remained to the present day.

the *parterre*

The parterre is a tradition characterised by patterns on the garden's surface. Essentially a feature, it is often viewed from a mount or raised platform which focuses attention on the formal pattern of its layout. Knot gardens, mazes and labyrinths of clipped box, myrtle or herbs, using plants with ornamental leaves rather than flowers, almost appear woven, like the raised pattern of a carpet spread across the garden. Though rather high maintenance because of the constant clipping involved, they display perfectly the idea of moulding and controlling nature with an elegance of dignified orderliness.

Draw your plan out on paper first, scaling up to the bed for planting and one may produce any pattern. In the sacred garden, a symbolic mandala pattern will last almost indefinitely and, through the necessary detailed and frequent clipping, provide an opportunity for meditation.

pagan

in praise of cosmic nature

Once holy places, the circles of stone found all over Europe and beyond are the most visible representatives of what we now call pagan belief. A sense of 'otherness' and accumulated sanctity pervades these places, unique expressions of the once understood power of nature. Cosmic symbolism ruled the religious rites of these ancient peoples and they built huge stone calendars and star maps of the rotation of the heavens, living monuments to mark the rising and setting of the sun and moon. At a time in human history when everything was controlled by and subject to the all-encompassing power of natural forces, the only reliable and enduring phenomena were to be seen in the sky. Constellations like the Great Bear were believed to be the hands of a gigantic celestial clock. The three stars in the tail point outward to the cardinal compass directions providing an indication of the seasons and fixing calculations for a calendar.

There is an important sense in which these pagan ideas are useful to us now. The perception of the sky has changed over the years. Step outside at night in the city and it's impossible to see the sky, masked as it is by the glow of street lights. Just once or twice on a distant holiday trip, we might get to see the real sky. To the ancient peoples, the sky appeared as an oppressive dome that appeared close above, full of more points of light than we can ever imagine. This is how the sky was seen on every cloudless night and so it is no wonder that it had such an impression.

A practical idea

A sundial in the garden, not only helps one to understand the sun's passage across the garden and therefore which areas may benefit, but also serves as a reminder of long-held visions of cosmic influence.

lunar *cycles and planting in the garden*

Perhaps surprisingly the garden is one of the most perfect vehicles for getting back in touch with ancient concepts and the lost valuable knowledge they contain. All life on earth evolves according to the cyclic nature of the heavens, especially the plants, which develop in response to the cues provided. The moon's cycles are the most obvious. The cycles of the moon have been observed to influence the speed of germination and the chances of success when transplanting, weeding and harvesting, and this is thought to be because of the changing effects of the moon's gravity as it moves relative to the earth and sun. At new moon, it lies between the earth and sun, and its gravity works together with that of the sun. When the moon is full, it is on the opposite side of the earth to the sun and their gravitational pulls tend to cancel each other out a bit. The two weeks of increasing moonlight and decreasing gravitational pull, from the new to full moon, stimulate leaf and above-ground growth. Conversely, root growth is stimulated when the moon is waning and its gravitational pull is beginning to work with that of the sun again.

Here are some suggestions for how to use the influence of the moon and test the theory of lunar planting for yourself. Take the new moon as your starting point:

Week 1– when lunar gravitational pull is decreasing and its light increasing, it is good for general and balanced growth.

Week 2 – when the moon is approaching full and its gravitational pull is nearly at its lowest, foliage growth and the planting of rapidly germinating, above-ground plants seeds, are favoured.

Week 3 – when both lunar gravity appears to be increasing and light is decreasing, root growth is favoured.

Week 4 – a period of rest, when the moon and sun are pulling in almost the same direction, and the moon's light is decreasing to its minimum.

When sowing for both root and leafy plant growth, two or three days prior to the phase peak, should be allowed for the seeds to take up water.

archetypal symbols

As our scientific understanding expands our world view has become increasingly more mechanical and dehumanised. Man is less involved with nature, breeding a sense of isolation. As our symbolic identification with nature decreases and our reliance on science increases, the emotional energy that we once drew from nature is lost. We no longer believe thunder to be the voice of an angry god, lightning his avenging messenger, or that rivers contain spirits. Trees no longer represent a life principle, and snakes no longer represent the embodiment wisdom. However, many superstitions still persist; the number thirteen, black cats and walking beneath ladders are still considered to be unlucky.

In our garden sanctuary, there are many symbols and creations that we can employ to preserve and bring to life a memory of those deeper and older connections. We may find it in the form of a particular plant or tree, a colour, a flower, a statue or ornament. Simply, in order to enhance the notion of a respite from the modern chaotic world, we can actively begin to restore our sense of place and, a deeper health and feeling of well-being within it through exploring our symbolic relationship to nature.

The fertility of the fields is one of the most enduring and powerful of all images. Symbolically, it represents more than just food. In the eastern faiths, many deities are depicted being born from flowers. The flowers are the symbols of all that is good and bountiful, of paradise, the fertile cosmos and the mysteries of the cycle of life.

We have often associated ourselves more easily with the upright stance of plants and trees than with the horizontal posture of the animals, and plants have come to symbolise the growth of all things on their way to enlightenment or heaven. Mythic beings have been thought to live in the plants, Hindu devas and fairies who sprinkle creation with their fertile magic.

the *sacred tree of life*

In seeking to give our lives meaning we have always looked to our environment and the things around us and, when searching for something to impress or inspire ourselves, it is no surprise that we have invested the tree with infinite credit. As the myths have grown, it is the tree that has come to represent the axis of the universe. The most powerful link between heaven and earth. Its summit touches the sky, carrying the highest of our aspirations, its roots, the foundation pillars of the world, deep, dark and unconscious, the source of all knowledge and enrichment. The tree is bountiful, beautiful, useful, a building material, a tool, a food, nourishing, shading and giving shelter to all creation.

In every mythology across time, from the Egyptian goddess Nut emerging from a sycamore fig to dispense the elixir of immortality, to the Scandinavian god's steed, Yggdrasil, the ash tree binding earth, heaven and hell. Every culture, every life, has been cradled, grounded and nurtured by these gentle giants. They form our landscapes, witness events and hold memories beyond our comprehension. The olive tree, mentioned in Genesis and venerated by Arab and Jew alike, is said to be the source of life. It symbolises Abraham to one belief, Muhammad's beautiful dream realisation to another. It was the founding tree of Athens, endowed with the power of rebirth and planted by Athena on the Acropolis.

The tree as a symbol of divine knowledge is central to many myths. Was that famous and oft-described fatal tempter an apple or a fig, a palm perhaps? Fabulous tales tell of the oak and the yew scattering the thoughts of the dead to the four winds. The Christmas Tree, still the spirit of fecundity in mid-winter, and Lindens the tree of peace and freedom from the yoke of tyranny. In the centuries-old tradition of the *Qabbalah*, the tree of life is a ladder to higher consciousness and we are asked to climb step by step, branch after branch to reach the crown of enlightenment.

Different flowers have separate meanings but in flower symbolism relies on the character or shape of the flower. Most often it is the archetypal image for the soul. Symbolic of the work of the sun, a transitory blossom is used to celebrate the joys of life and the ephemeral nature of pleasure. The tradition of throwing flowers over bodies and graves is an analogy for the flower's life and its passing.

A consensus of the many different traditions ascribing symbolism to flower colour denotes that orange and yellow are sun symbols, with red representing the relationship to animal life, blood and passion. Blue is a symbol of the impossible, an allusion to the mystic centre of the Grail perhaps, something to be striven for yet unattainable in earthly life. White represents all that is good and pure, ourselves transported to divine consciousness

personification – statues and the green man

we are the world in miniature

From classical statues of gods or god-like characters, heroes and heroines, even the elfin garden gnome, every individual personification contains within it the idea of the 'universal human'. A man and woman depicted together acts as the symbol for opposites, good and bad, high and low, cold and hot, wet and dry: a seed containing the totality of being. Expressed by the alchemists as sulphur and mercury this pairing was thought to be the metal scaffolding with which to build the foundations of life.

The human figure is often used to symbolise the microcosm within the macrocosm and the complete range of possibilities that are open to us. Imagine that you are another world in miniature, the sun and moon and the stars and you will understand the archetypal symbol of the human form. Halfway between heaven and earth, the head corresponds to the heavens, the breath to air, the belly to the sea and the lower parts to earth.

The attitudes or positions which the body assumes are highly significant: the cross, with arms outstretched, the union of the worlds; the squatting position of the Buddha and Norse gods, the renunciation of the baser parts of our nature. As a classic icon, the Buddha does not represent one person or a god, but a nature, a personality and a discipline for us to observe and pursue.

the *green man*

One of the oldest, most diffused and potent bodies of myth and folklore surrounds the idea of a 'man-in-the-trees'. In all his manifestations he possesses the characteristic of elusiveness, a power of melting into the trees. There is a strange attraction of this myth, so profound and universal, because he represents our deepest, now largely unconscious, connection to the wild.

Adopted by the Church in the Middle Ages, the foliate mask symbol dates back to a much older pagan period. They have been found in Roman art of the first century and early examples of a semi-human peering through a frond of leaves appear on the walls of temples or as tomb decorations. In medieval times he is associated with the 'Woodwose' or spirit of the forest, and in the spring his likeness would be carried through the streets to shouts of 'The Green Man is here!' His adorning leaves were later removed and buried in the crop fields to bring fertility.

In the sixteenth and seventeenth centuries the Green Man, decked with twigs, would appear in pageants. Known as 'whifflers', these characters cleared the way for the procession; today in the

Austrian Alps, folklore characters known as 'whifflers' appear at spring fairs to chase away the winter with a sweeping broom.

In our garden sanctuary the image of a Green Man is a potent symbol, a reminder of the true wildness of nature, its seeming transience, both creative ferment and hidden potential. It is a reminder that man is connected deep in our psyches, and that the wildness disappears if ever it is merely classified or relegated to the past. It is the antithesis to order: chaotic and at its most base murmuring, untameable, wild and free.

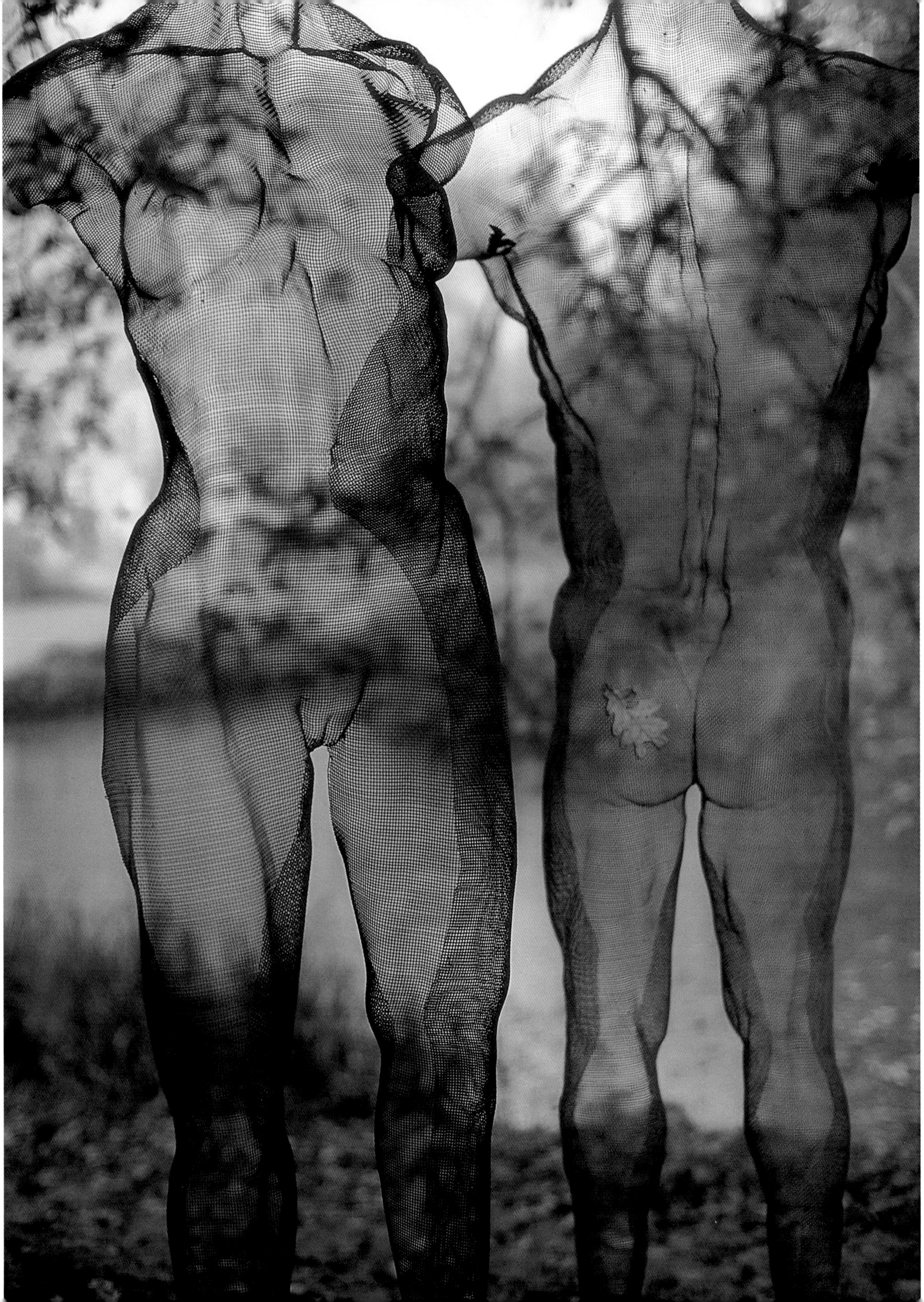

the universe in shapes

the circle and ultimate wholeness

The circle is the sign of ultimate wholeness and an emblem for the relationship between humankind and the whole of nature. The sphere, has always been seen to represent the disc of the life-giving sun and that crucial invention, the wheel. From ancient observers to today's satellite image of the earth, it is the 360-degree view of our home and the heavens. C.G.Jung, the psychologist, said the circle was the ultimate symbol of the self. From primitive sun worship, through myths and dreams to the sacred mandala meditation tool of Tibetan monks, the circle is truly universal. Through every culture, every religion, metaphysical belief and scientific reason, the cyclic notion of life, the universe and all within it, makes the circle the most enduring and profound of symbols.

deep *connections to the universal mind*

Just to draw a circle in the sand is to make a connection to a universal mind that has existed since the beginning of time. The many ways of dividing the circle then lead us to open a massive emporium of cultural icons and metaphysical representations. One of the oldest is the idea of two halves, a dark and a light. The notion of opposites contained within the circle, called Yin and Yang by the Chinese. This emblem evolves very easily into a great many of the eastern meditation figures known as Yantras or mandalas. These are aids to focus, stimulate and calm the mind, geometric in design and embellishing the circle with triangles, squares and extending angles and rays. There are also splendid western examples in the rose windows of cathedrals and mosques. Think of stone circles, sun wheels, astronomical solar and lunar orientation temples. The circle enters every aspect of classical, medieval and modern design and the temple designer and the town planner have each sought to extend its potential and its symbolism. Those embellishments reached a peak during the Middle Ages, when the alchemists in their symbolic and mathematical attempts to find ways to 'square the circle', expressed the spiritual and scientific quest of their time.

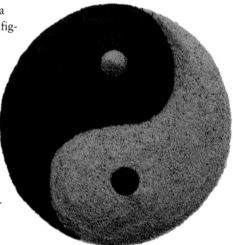

planet *earth, a modern symbol*

In recent years, everyone has been impressed by the highly evocative view of the Earth taken from space: the beautiful blue-green planet. It has become a modern icon, the circle imbued with all of the meaning of a symbol that deeply involves us, now, on this little sphere revolving in space.

future symbols – a new aesthetic

outer and inner space

The last one hundred years witnessed many new discoveries which have dramatically quickened the pace of evolution. Perhaps the most fruitful development has been the broadening of our imagination with help from two traditionally conflicting directions. Science and metaphysics, with their roots in such contrastingly different parts of human culture, are seeming to converge, creating a fascinating dialogue. Discoveries in physics, of quantum and 'string' theories, have allowed advances in astronomy that allow us to see objects that are millions of light years back in time. Such developments lead us to question who, what and where we are. The glimpses of microscopic life that the electron microscope and the computer have given us, dramatise further the contrast between the outer and, the infinitely smaller inner space. Witnessing the results of these technological advances, we are awed at the enormity and diversity of nature herself.

We now understand that what we see as plants and trees, rocks, sand, water and air, are in fact bodies of vibrating molecules and atoms interacting with each other. They appear chaotic and randomly associated, yet they are acting, almost consciously with some specialised signature of form and movement that makes them quite unique as flowers, petals, a gas or mineral. Beginning to grasp these concepts and yet feeling a sense of almost religious awe is what informs the huge leap in imagination that we are all experiencing. An exciting and new aesthetic is appearing at the end of the twentieth century. You don't have to be a nuclear physicist or a Zen monk to appreciate it.

a mandala *for our times*

As the final symbol in this section, which in some way we may wish to include in our modern idea of a garden sanctuary, I offer one of the most futuristic, a mandala that embodies the spirit of our times, the Fractal image. Fritjof Capra's *Tao of Physics* explains this concept: 'the influence of modern physics goes way beyond technology. It extends to the realm of thought and culture, where it has led to a deep revision of our concept of the universe and our relationship to it.' The image here is a complicated mathematically generated computer model. Without the technology we cannot hope to recreate it. What it demonstrates, however, is that an object can be created from what appears to be total chaos, the seemingly random action of innumerable factors all acting on one another at the same time. Our previously fragmented view, that each thing is separate from every other thing, each part to be exploited differently, is beginning to evolve, the edges are blurring, into a more holistic view, showing that the 'parts' are 'part of the whole'. We are beginning to be aware of the unity and mutual interrelation of all things, the implication for us is that we may now transcend the notion of an isolated individual self and begin to identify with a more universal reality.

We are beginning to understand how everything is connected to everything else, including us. Dynamical systems like the weather are composed of so many interacting elements that they are tremendously sensitive to the tiniest influence. The heat rising from a street of cars, the wind from the wings of a mosquito in Madagascar, almost anything not included in the meteorologist's measurements could change the behaviour of a whole weather system.

creating the space

One step at a time

If there were an an ideal world, the perfect, self-sustaining garden would be laid out and growing the way we planned and dreamed. Life and nature is not like that! This chapter combines the ideas discussed throughout the book to form an archetypal garden sanctuary. Before creating your own garden sanctuary it is essential to stand back for a while and observe, noting what already exists. It is much easier to work within an existing framework, than to change everything immediately. You may decide to use these ideas to form a plan for the whole garden, or perhaps just for a special feature in one area.

Your 'intent' is everything

Experiment with the ideas contained within this book – your ultimate aim should be to create a garden that makes you feel good! It might be that a certain traditional ceremonial chant has sounds within its original language that precisely affect different vibrational parts of the body and mind. However, if this language does not mean something to you, change the word to reflect your personal beliefs. The ceremony of the Agnihotre (*see page 25*) is a good example. The sole intention of the ceremony is to symbolically clean the air and assist with the absorption of nutrients. One can recite the Hindu chant, but we are creating a modern sacred concept, where your 'intention' is just as important. Feel free to create your own poetry, your own chant. It is your 'intention' that will make it work for you.

north

Water and blue
The climate is cold
The winter solstice

The area of your garden that faces north is the area of blue, of the element water, and of wavy, meandering shapes. This quarter will include your water features, a stream, fountain, bird bath or pond. Herbal plants and flowers here are used to energise our bones, kidneys, bladder and ears. Plants with medicinal or aromatic properties that assist the healing of fear are favoured. Also, think of placing a symbol for winter in this area.

Blue plant suggestions
For wildlife – Buddleia, Lilac, Hyssop
For perfume – Clematis
For display – *Meconopsis* blue poppy, Campanula, Bluebells
For healing – Borage, Sweet violet, Forget-me-not, Lavender, Sage, Rosemary, Alliums, Lady's mantle
For taste – Thyme, Cabbage, Globe artichoke, Damson
Suggested garden feature – The Flow Form waterfall. An undulating, surrounding blue border.

An archetypal garden sanctuary

An archetypal garden design that combines many common traditional themes, can be based on the natural calendar as it appears in the 'Seasonal Gardens' chapter. Each of the cardinal compass directions or quarters of the garden, should include the relevant colours, aromas, sounds and elemental materials (water, earth, wood, fire and metal) associated with that part of the garden. Chosen evocative images and symbolic features, alongside the appropriate healing plants, will stimulate and focus the mind and body. Using the garden as a vehicle for a daily meditation, visit each area in turn, celebrating and experiencing the nature of those elements, inviting them to participate in daily life. Do this for half an hour a day, perhaps twice, morning and evening, and watch your life change. Your health will improve and your stress levels reduced.

north east

Earth and yellow
The climate is damp
and humid
Imbolc

In the north east the colour is yellow, of earth. The shapes favoured are horizontal and square. Stone ornaments, statues, ceramic pots or moss-covered boulders may be placed here to represent the earth. Plants and flowers used to energise the stomach, spleen, muscles and mouth are recommended. Other plants with medicinal or aromatic properties to heal worry may be included. In the very early part of spring, the symbolic keynote of this area, the awakening must be calm and assured.

Yellow plant suggestions
For wildlife – Honeysuckle, Daffodil, Buttercup, Sunflower, Goldenrod
For perfume – Santolina, Wallflower, Witch hazel
For display – Primrose, Geum
For healing – Evening primrose, Marigold, Heartsease, Agrimony, Fennel, Yellow gentian
For taste – Bay, Pumpkin, Lovage
Suggested garden features – Statue or sculpture symbolising awakening. Square flag-stone path alternated with shallow square beds and pot plantings.

east

Wood and dark green
The climate is of wind
The spring equinox

The eastern area of the garden represents movement and encompasses the element of wood and the colour dark green. Include woody plants, a wooden viewing deck or platform, wooden seats or chairs and any wooden containers, barrels or plant boxes, even your fuel wood pile. This quarter has the climate of wind and so you may wish to symbolise this lighter optimistic element with wind chimes. As green is the colour, this may be the area for a lawn on which to play spring-like outgoing and joyful games.

Green woody plant suggestions
For wildlife – Holly, Nettles,
For perfume – Lemon balm, Mahonia
For display – Ivy, Box, Male fern, Conifers
For healing – Elder, Angelica
For taste – Broad beans, Horseradish, Gooseberry, Tarragon
Suggested garden features – Wooden viewing deck with Ivy and Male fern as a backdrop on a fanned frame behind. Topiaried box in tubs. A hard-wearing, meadow-turf semi-circular fan-shaped lawn with a small shrub border. Bamboo soft wind chimes.

south east

Wind
Beltane festival

In the south east is the second wood and lighter green area. Rectangular shapes, new plantings and juicy young stems are favoured here. The outward spring energy takes on more structure, expanding further with new growth in the ascendant. Medicinal and aromatic plants to energise the liver, gallbladder, eyes and tendons are recommended, alongside plants to heal anger.

Green young and juicy plant suggestions

For wildlife – Ground covering Ivy (*Hedera helix*), Chickweed in a container

For perfume – *Nicotiana*, Dames Violet

For display – Sea Kale, Acanthus, Hostas, Myrtle

For healing – Basil, Feverfew, Eyebright, Skullcap

For taste – Chives, Purslane, Sorrel, Endive, Lamb's lettuce

Suggested garden features – A Chamomile seat; a rectangular tub or brick surround filled with earth and planted. A young green leaf border.

south

Fire and red
The climate is of heat
The summer solstice

The area of the garden that faces south represents fire, the colour red, and upward sharp, pointed shapes. Flames are the perfect image and so it is here that you may wish to site a fire or barbecue. Lighting effects or reflective surfaces will also project light into this pattern or shape. Prisms also direct and reflect light in sharp and pointed rays. Those medicinal or aromatic plants are favoured which energise the heart, blood vessels, the small intestine and tongue. As summer is the season of abundance this is the perfect area for a meal table for the joy of feasting and partying. The whole area is alive and invigorated with colour and scent alongside the action of the fire and flames.

Red plant suggestions
For wildlife – Flowering thorn, Quince, Cherry, Sedum, Pennyroyal, Saxifrage
For perfume – *Rosa* x *damascena*, Rose geranium, Jasmine, Passion flower, Artemesia
For display – Smoke bush, Hibiscus, Camellia, Campion, Scarlet pimpernel
For healing – Echinacea, Impatiens, Bergamot, Peony, Dog rose, Centaury, Red valerian, Sweet Marjoram, Thyme, Clary sage
For taste – Tomatoes, Runner beans, Red currants, *Lollo Rosso*
Suggested garden features – Fire pit or red brick barbecue with Chamomile seat one side, stone seat on the opposite side and central meal table. A high level border.

south west

Earth and orange
Climate is damp and humid
The festival of Lugnasadh

The south west features earth, more intensely this time as it is linked with the colour orange. The shape and movement is predominately sideways and you might embody this with ground-covering plants, especially if they are healing to the stomach, muscles or mouth. It is the place of late summer and a yellow-orange fruit would symbolise it perfectly. As stone is also indicated, another sculpture, a rock or a stone seat may provide another place of nourishment and clarity.

Orange plant suggestions
For wildlife – Buttercup, Winter aconite, Marsh marigold
For perfume – Mexican orange blossom, Cotton lavender, Agrimony
For display – Japanese maple, *Crocosmia* 'Lucifer'
For healing – St John's wort, Nasturtium, Witch hazel
For taste – Sunflower, Anise, Nasturtium, Cowslip, Coriander
Suggested garden features – A rock or a stone seat and a bed of ground-covering St John's wort, Nasturtium and *Crocosmia* 'Lucifer'

west

Metal and white & silver
The climate is dry
The autumn equinox

The western quarter of the garden represents the element metal together with the colours white and silver. As the climate of metal is dry, this area is perhaps the best for a dry garden. A sculpted quarter will include the most base mineral elements of crystal and white, stone gravel or chippings, speckled with small pieces of found metal. Opposite wood and the viewing deck or wooden seat, this prime outlook may employ the Zen techniques of 'combing' or raking the chippings into sweeping patterns. Crystalline rock boulders placed in the centre of the design to look like islands in the sea, will create the gathering inward and contemplative image.

White plant suggestions
For wildlife – Blackberry, Hawthorn
For perfume – Gardenia, Madonna lily, *Jasminum officinale*, winter-flowering Honeysuckle, Solomon's Seal
For display – Snowdrop, Campanula, *Dicentra examina* 'Alba'
For healing – Daisy, Hops, Wild garlic, Chamomile, Yarrow, Chickweed, Meadow saffron, Alliums
For taste – Sweet cicely, Apple
Suggested garden features – A wrought-iron apple arbour with a hawthorn end and metal urns underneath. The border of white flowers.

north west

Metal and white & gold
The climate is dry
The Samhain festival

The north west contains the second expression of metal and white. A wrought-iron arbour suggests the covered and inward nature of the quarter, with a climbing white flowering rose or winter flowering honeysuckle. Metal here may move to copper and gold, a mirror perhaps or a bronze urn tumbling with white flowers. Medicinal and aromatic plants will energise the lungs, intestine, skin and nose, their essence will heal grief and darkness and give strength and courage. This is the final element in the cycle and gives deep mineral nutrients to all the other elements. This area may be a good place for a compost heap which, like the season represented here, produces the foundation, the structure and the building blocks for life.

A daily garden meditation

For a daily garden meditation, lay out a circle of stones like a Medicine Wheel. Pick up each stone in the circle in turn. Each stone represents an element and cardinal point. Take the stone to its own area of the garden. Walk around or sit by in that area. Do some digging, weeding or planting. The simplest method to engage your attention is to acknowledge that element, think about its attributes, its qualities and how many times it appears in nature. Then celebrate the part that it plays in the natural order. Replace this stone and move clockwise to the next, repeating the process. Finish with the life-giving energies of the centre stones, the sun and moon, here representing matter and spirit. The prayer is for them to combine.

Further reading

Too, Lillian, *Lillian Too's Basic Feng Shui*, Konsep Books, 1997
ISBN 983-9778-05-6
One of the best introductory books.

Harper, Peter, *The Natural Garden Book*, Gaia Books, 1994
ISBN 1-85675-056-6
Explains the basics of natural gardening.

Whitefield, Patrick, *How to make a Forest Garden,* Permanent
Publications, 1996
ISBN 1-85623-008-2

Bennett, Jackie, *The Wildlife Garden Month by Month*
David & Charles, 1997
ISBN 0-7153-0573-5

Fern, Ken, *Plants for a Future,* Permanent Publications, 1997
ISBN 1-85623-011-2
Edible and useful plants, a book to change the world!

Tompkins, Pete, and Bird, Christopher, *Secrets of the Soil,*
Penguin/Arkana, 1989
ISBN 0-14-019311-1
A fascinating book on bio-dynamic ideas, with facts about
nature and growing.

Hamilton, Geoff, *Geoff Hamilton's Paradise Gardens,*
BBC Books, 1997
ISBN 0-563-38414-X
Almost anything by Geoff will inspire.

Stevens, David, *The Garden Design Sourcebook,* Conran
Octopus, 1995
ISBN 1-85029-7320
One of the best manuals on many aspects of garden design.

Minter, Sue, *The Healing Garden,* Headline Books, 1994
ISBN 0-7472-7914-4
A good introduction to herbals and healing by the curator of
the Chelsea Physic Garden.

Caddy, Eileen, *Opening Doors Within,* Findhorn Press, 1987
ISBN 0-905249-68-2
Daily thoughts which really do help.

Suppliers and organisations

PLANTS FOR A FUTURE
Ken Fern, The Field, Penpol, Lostwithiel, Cornwall,
PL22 0NG
Tel: 01208 873554
Data base with information on all aspects of care for
plants in temperate climates. Over 6500 species listed.

THE ROYAL HORTICULTURAL SOCIETY PLANT CENTRE
RHS Garden, Wisley, Woking, Surrey GU23 6QB
Tel: 01483 211113

HENRY DOUBLEDAY RESEARCH ASSOCIATION
Ryton Gardens, Ryton On Dunsmore, Coventry, CV8 3LG
Tel: 01203 303517
The best organic research centre in Britain, includes
seed banks for traditional and endangered species.

CHILTERN SEEDS
Bortree Stile, Ulverston, Cumbria, LA12 7PB
Tel: 01229 581137
Over 4000 species listed in an excellent catalogue.

AGRO-FORESTRY RESEARCH TRUST
17 Arden Drive, Chelston, Torquay, Devon, TQ2 6DZ
Advice on woodland gardens, food and other
commodities. Quarterly magazine.

THE GREEN SHOP
Bisley, Stroud, Glos. GL6 7BX
Tel: 01452 770629
www.greenshop.co.uk
For a huge variety of alternative technology
commodities e.g. water systems. Catalogue and
website for advice.

SOCIETY OF HOMOEOPATHS
2 Artizan Road, Northampton, NN1 4HV
Tel: 01604 621400
For finding a practitioner and advice in your area.

BIODYNAMIC SUPPLIERS LTD
Woodman Lane, Clent, Stourbridge, West Midlands,
DY9 9PX
Suppliers of organic materials, equipment, recipes
for fertilisers and compost preparations, disease and
pest control.

SUFFOLK HERBS LTD
Sawyers Farm, Little Cornard, Sudbury, Suffolk CO10 0NY
Tel: 01376 572456
Suppliers of seeds, stock and materials.

CHASE ORGANICS
Coomberlands House, Coomberlands Lane, Addlestone,
Surrey, KT15 1HY
Tel: 01932 253666
Seeds catalogue, materials and equipment.

CULPEPPER LTD
21 Bruton Street, Berkeley Square, London, W1X 7OA
Tel: 020 7629 4559
Herbal remedies.

THE SACRED GARDEN COMPANY
54 Duke Street, Cheltenham, GL52 6BP
Tel: 01242 570219
Garden and landscape design, advice and information
on all aspects of natural gardening and growing.

Index